Etsy

GW00457233

TABLE OF CONTENTS

ETSY

Magnificent production, easy to make

CINDY J. LOAN

© **Copyright 2021 - All rights reserved.**

The content contained within this book may not be reproduced, duplicated or transmitted without direct written permission from the author or the publisher.

Under no circumstances will any blame or legal responsibility be held against the publisher, or author, for any damages, reparation, or monetary loss due to the information contained within this book. Either directly or indirectly.

Legal Notice:

This book is copyright protected. This book is only for personal use. You cannot amend, distribute, sell, use, quote or paraphrase any part, or the content within this book, without the consent of the author or publisher.

Disclaimer Notice:

Please note the information contained within this document is for educational and entertainment purposes only. All effort has been executed to present accurate, up to date, and reliable, complete information. No warranties of any kind are declared or implied. Readers acknowledge that the author is not engaging in the rendering of legal, financial, medical or professional advice. The content within this book has been derived from various sources. Please consult a licensed professional before attempting any techniques outlined in this book.

By reading this document, the reader agrees that under no circumstances is the author responsible for any losses, direct or indirect, which are incurred as a result of the use of information contained within this document, including, but not limited to, — errors, omissions, or inaccuracies.

About Cindy

Craft business expert Cindy J. Loan writes for those who want a profitable, creative lifestyle.

What Cindy has accomplished:

--Marketed more than 200 handmade products at highly competitive art and craft fairs, in galleries from New York's Soho district to the Grand Canyon, and online at Etsy and Amazon.

--Started and ran a gallery-gift shop selling art and crafts near one of America's top tourist destinations, Santa Fe, NM.

--Produced and presented craft business courses for the University of Rome, The Learning Annex, Sageways, and the Boot Camp Marketing for Artists.

--Coached clients on how to grow their craft business getting publicity on top-tier TV shows including the Today Show, MSNBC, Success Magazine, and others.

--

--Authored sixteen books, interviewed in major media including The Wall Street Journal, Family Circle, Working Mothers and top-tier consumer magazines.

What real people are saying about Cindy.....

"Cindy is by far the most qualified and talented marketer for the craft industry. Her knowledge is only outweighed by her honest desire to help people." - Phoebe Vinces, Vice President, Palmi Inc.

Preface

Etsy-preneurship consists of the knowledge and tools needed to start and run a business on Etsy—turning a hobby into a thriving business. Since 2007, I have helped thousands of Etsy sellers start their Etsy businesses, perform their bookkeeping, fulfill their tax obligations, operate with efficiency, market their products, and run legal businesses. *Etsy-preneurship* is the resource that gives you all of this and more!

I've packed as much valuable content and tools into one book as possible! It is my aim that this book will be a resource for both Etsy newbies and Etsy veterans. I hope that Etsy newbies can shorten their steep learning curve and that Etsy veterans can find some fresh ways to improve their business.

If someone were to ask me what he or she needs to know to run a successful business on Etsy, my answer would be, "The contents of *Etsy-preneurship.*" *Etsy-preneurship* provides a firm foundation on which to build a business—one that will last and be profitable and rewarding.

Chapter 1, "Etsy + Entrepreneurship = Etsy-preneurship" is centered on the selling venue Etsy.com and the skills needed to be an entrepreneur. *Etsy-preneurship* is the business foundation you need to succeed. First, you have to start the foundation, as outlined in Chapter 2, "Creating a Business Plan," that will focus your business on the things that are most important. Then it is time to zero in on the six core foundations needed to run a successful business: "Bookkeeping" (Chapter 3), "Taxes" (Chapter 4), "Finances" (Chapter 5), "Legal" (Chapter 6), "Operations" (Chapter 7), and "Marketing" (Chapter 8). Next, the foundation is built stronger by using the information in Chapter 9, "Etsy Community: 40 Etsy Tips, Tricks, and Nuggets," which includes various important business topics. In Chapter 10, "Practicing Business Self-Development," I share the best resources and apps for Etsy sellers. Finally, Chapter 11, "Encouragement and Next Steps," provides help to turn all your knowledge and tools into a successful business. For Etsy sellers who are looking for additional ways to maximize their opportunities for success, I have included two advanced application studies: "Etsy Shop Ratios" (Study 1) and "Etsy Marketplace Trends That Impact Your Business" (Study 2). Every chapter includes valuable downloads (spreadsheets, forms, lists, and e-books) that help you easily apply what you have learned in that chapter in practical ways. *Etsy-preneurship* is your road map to a thriving Etsy business!

It is my desire to empower you with knowledge and tools to achieve your dreams on Etsy. You can do it!

Chapter 1 The World of Etsy

Etsy.com is a place where e-commerce has a heart. Since 2005, Etsy has been, and continues to be, the place to buy and sell handmade, vintage, and craft supplies. It is a community of commerce—crafters, artists, entrepreneurship, hipsters, nerds, moms, dads, grandmas, grandpas, kids, and collectives all call Etsy their home. Etsy is where creativity and commerce are linked together, and opportunities for businesses are ripe!

According to its website, Etsy's mission statement is " . . . to empower people to change the way the global economy works. We see a world in which very-very small businesses have much-much more sway in shaping the economy, local living economies are thriving everywhere, and people value authorship and provenance as much as price and convenience. We are bringing heart to commerce and making the world more fair, more sustainable, and more fun."

I personally know the power that Etsy brings to individuals who call Etsy their virtual storefront. Etsy provides freedom to succeed or fail in a business venture without breaking the bank. Crafters used to rely only on craft shows and boutiques to sell their products; while these are still important sales diversification revenue streams, Etsy opens the door to building something better. Etsy gives you a way to make sales around the world, build your business brand, and do it in a safe and encouraging environment. Selling on Etsy usually starts as a microbusiness, but can quickly grow into something more.

Etsy is booming! In just the one month of December 2011, more than 3.3 million items were sold on Etsy—with a value of $69.8 million! In that month, about 789,000 new members joined Etsy. The worldwide economy is hungry for commerce that is different. People are tired of giving gifts that are corporate-cookie-cutter look-alikes. Handmade and vintage is unique, original, and memorable. Behind every handmade and vintage item is a person—a person with passion and a story—not assembly lines, manufacturers, or corporate identities.

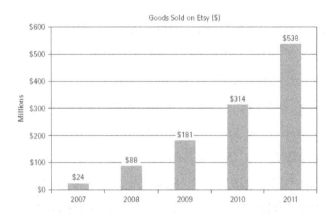

Goods Sold on Etsy ($)

Etsy's popularity is not slowing down. If you are or plan to be an Etsy seller, now is the time to claim your percentage of this market share. Creativity and quality are rewarded with success. Thousands of unclaimed craft and vintage niches are waiting for sellers to control, but creativity, crafting ability, and passion take you only so far—to be a lasting success, an Etsy seller must have a solid business foundation. Without a strong entrepreneurial foundation, Etsy businesses are not sustainable.

Starting a Business

Starting a business is not only for those individuals who have an MBA, hang out with venture capitalists, or are extreme risk takers. I firmly believe that most people should be small business owners at some point in their lives! Every person has creativity and untapped potential to make the world a better place through their respective businesses. In fact, I believe every person has a role in the global economy's future success by starting and running his or her own small business.

Starting and running your own business is an exciting adventure—it shows your passion. Etsy sellers start their businesses for a variety of reasons, including:

- The need for a productive and creative crafting outlet
- To make additional money to pay off debt, save for a vacation, or achieve other financial goals
- To take the first step toward quitting their day job
- To work for themselves
- Because they love buying things on Etsy and think they can sell, too!

There are just as many reasons for starting an Etsy business as there are Etsy sellers. No matter what your reasons are, I'm here to tell you, "Go for it! You can do it!" I've helped thousands of sellers start legal, legitimate, and sustainable businesses on Etsy, and I'm going to help you do it, too. Starting and running a business can be a little intimidating, but the way to overcome this fear is with the proper knowledge, tools, and guidance. I take great joy in empowering others to create businesses that are sustainable, thriving, and provide joy for years to come. I will teach you the art and science of Etsy-preneurship!

Etsy Basics

Etsy + entrepreneurship = Etsy-preneurship. This is the formula for the operational success of your business. Etsy-preneurship is the adventure you are about to embark on or are currently embracing.

Since 2007, I've been in conversation with every type of Etsy seller that seems to exist, selling everything imaginable, all unique and different. Not so unique are the business-related questions I am asked. Most Etsy sellers have the crafting side of their business down well. I am always amazed at the new items I see for sale on Etsy! You already have the "Etsy" part of the formula—amazing crafting, artistic, and design skills. Of course, there are components to this side of your business that you may want to improve on. If you are like most Etsy sellers, you are more confident in your crafting abilities than in your business skills.

The "Entrepreneurship" part of this formula includes the business foundations that make your creations soar! Over the years, through hearing and answering thousands of Etsy sellers' business-related questions, I know what it takes to build a successful business on Etsy. I have created a model, or method, on which businesses can thrive! My motto has always been, "Helping your Etsy shop thrive!" I want to help *your* business thrive!

The Model

The Etsy-preneurship model will help your Etsy shop thrive! The following topics will help you build a firm business foundation, which will create success for you and your business. Tips and tricks are helpful, but a rock-solid foundation will help you build a business that will last. Each chapter of the remainder of this book corresponds to the following Etsy-preneurship model.

Etsy-preneurship:
The Business Foundation

	Bookkeeping	Legal	
Handmade Business Plan →	Taxes	Operations	← Practicing Business Self-Development
Starting the foundation	Finances	Marketing	*Developing the foundation*

↑
Community: Etsy Tips, Tricks, and Nuggets
Building the foundation

Creating an Initial Plan

If you do not have an initial business plan, you are setting yourself up to fail. A business plan gives you a fighting chance at success. Planning in your head is not good enough. The process of putting it into written words really does make a difference, because it often shows so-called good ideas to be impractical and helps develop weak ideas into blockbusters of success.

Bookkeeping

The first time you spend or receive your money related to your business, a transaction has occurred and the need for bookkeeping has begun. Etsy sellers who sweep this administrative task under the rug to worry about later are asking for trouble. Good, simple, and practical bookkeeping systems help Etsy sellers are able to better price their products, make smarter business decisions, and meet tax obligations that all Etsy sellers face.

Death and Taxes

Death and taxes—you know the spiel! All Etsy sellers have tax obligations, even if they consider their business a hobby! The tax law may seem confusing, but it is manageable in bite-sized pieces.

I will help you cut through to the parts that impact most Etsy sellers and explain the tax code in everyday language. As a CPA, the tax code is something I read regularly. It isn't always fun, but it is necessary. Having a basic understanding of the tax laws that face your business will make you feel more confident, especially when an IRS agent is sitting across from you asking about your Etsy business during an audit!

Finances

Running a successful business is dependent upon making good financial decisions. The way you manage your cash, bank accounts, PayPal account, and budgeting is just as important as performing your craft with great skill. I will reveal financial tips to help your business thrive, as well as the financial nightmares that you can easily avoid with a little foresight.

Run your Etsy Business—legally!

There is only one way to run your Etsy business—legally! Knowing the law gives you confidence to run a business well. There are legal implications regarding how you form your business, contracts you enter, and business insurance. Intellectual property (copyrights, trademarks, patents) are a hot topic for Etsy sellers. The law protects you, your business, and your creations. Legal knowledge empowers you and your business.

Day-to-Day Activities

Operations are the day-to-day activities that make up your business. Consistency and standards are your friends when dealing with shipping, producing your products, photographing your products, managing your Etsy shop, managing your inventory, scheduling, and more. Solid operations set clear expectations for you and your customers to rely on. Stable operations that are sustainable will help prevent you and your business from burning out.

Marketing Basics

Just because you list your product on Etsy does not mean it will automatically sell. Sometimes this happens, but it is not the norm. Marketing is where creativity gets to shine, but without the proper marketing framework and disciplines, your business will be all over the place and without focus. Marketing is an art that requires a little science to make its impact most effective.

Etsy Community: Etsy Tips, Trics.

The Etsy community is special. Most of the corporate business world is a dog-eat-dog environment, but the Etsy community is different. Etsy sellers help other Etsy sellers—yes, even direct competitors sometimes help direct competitors! Relying on the communal tips, advice, and wisdom from those who have gone before you and are in the same journey with you is a treasure chest of gold nuggets! Together, we will begin digging into these tips, advice, and wisdom and explore where to find more.

Practicing Business Self-Development

The fact that you are reading this book shows that you value developing yourself and your business. You must grow personally in the components you already know about business. This does not happen magically, but rather with intentionality. Business self-development is the water, fertilizer, and fertile soil that will help your business grow faster. It will also help you avoid costly mistakes. Together, we will look at the most helpful resources available for Etsy sellers.

Next Steps and Advanced Application Studies

Finally, you will be encouraged by the stories of a few Etsy sellers, and you can plan your next steps toward creating a thriving business. I have also included two advanced application studies that can help both newbie and experienced Etsy sellers improve their business by looking within their own shop and at the Etsy marketplace as a whole.

My Etsy-preneurship Story

My wife, Katie, started selling on Etsy in 2007, thus beginning her Etsy-preneurship story. She loves babies, had worked with babies in her job, and naturally started making baby-related handmade products. She sewed burp cloths, baby bibs, diaper bags, and the cutest little baby girl dresses and jackets! She started her Etsy shop as a way to be able to work from home and not take on a full-time job. During this time, we were saving money to purchase our first home, with hopes of soon expanding our own family with little ones to use all these cute things, too!

During this time, we learned our way around Etsy: buying raw materials, making products, taking pictures, writing product descriptions, pricing products, shipping products, and all the other fun Etsy activities (posting in the forums, Etsy blogs, and Etsy teams). It did not take long to realize, "Whoa, we are starting our own business here! What about the legal requirements of running our own business? What about the tax implications? What will we use for a bookkeeping system? Oh, we need a business plan, too! And wait, we don't even have a business-only bank account! What will our day-to-day operations look like?" This is where my Etsy-preneurship story begins.

I have an undergraduate degree in accounting and a master's degree in accountancy from Baylor University. I am a Certified Public Accountant (CPA) and Certified Treasury Professional (CTP). I have worked as an international accountant, financial reporting manager, and treasury professional. I have also always been passionate about finance and entrepreneurship—saving money in a tiny jar at the encouragement of my grannie at a young age, buying candy and marking it up for a profit as a freshman in high school, and, with a friend, starting and running a lawn care service in high school and college. Business and finances are part of who I am, and I saw an opportunity to help my wife make her business succeed.

I started out by building a bookkeeping system to help her keep track of her sales, purchases, and inventory. We started using it to track her finances, and then I had my "aha" moment: If my wife needed this bookkeeping system, other Etsy sellers did, too. I made the system a little more user-friendly and robust and opened my own Etsy shop to sell it to other Etsy sellers. The shop's name is JJMFinance, where I still sell and am part of the Etsy community.

The first time I listed my bookkeeping system on Etsy, I was nervous! I remember looking at the pictures, reading the description over and over, wondering whether what I was putting up there was good enough. A few days later, it sold! I was so excited! After a few more days, I received my first positive feedback. I was hooked!

I began reading Etsy sellers' business-related questions in the forums and answering them. Then I started getting more *convos* (conversations, or messages from Etsy sellers) with various business questions. Soon, I started creating more products to help address these additional business questions.

I got involved with Handmadeology.com ("The Science of Handmade"), which helps Etsy sellers run their business. Also, I am a contributing editor for Handmadeology Pro, a member-only site that provides instructional videos, e-books, and spreadsheet tools to Etsy sellers.

I also provide business advice for Etsy sellers through Etsy-preneurship.com and my related Etsy shop, Epreneurship.

This is my Etsy-preneurship story over the past six years. I love Etsy and Etsy sellers!

Instructions for Etsy-preneurship.com and Accessing Digital Downloads

Each chapter in this book has one or more digital downloads that can be downloaded at etsy-preneurship.com. On this site, each chapter has a specific web page with information outlining that chapter's topic, including videos, useful links, downloadable spreadsheet tools, and other helpful information. Accessing this information is paramount to completing your study of Etsy-preneurship. When prompted, as you are downloading each chapter's supplement, simply enter the password located in the back of your book. As you read through this book, here are the steps I suggest you follow:

1. Read a chapter.

2. View the specific web page for that chapter on www.etsy-preneurship.com to watch related videos, read supplemental material, and become more knowledgeable about the specific business foundation you are learning about.

3. Download the chapter's supplemental content (spreadsheet, printable PDF form, or e-book)—

available at www.etsy-preneurship.com/downloads.

4. Work through the supplemental content, and then proceed with the same steps for the next chapter, working your way through the entire book.

All spreadsheets are designed for use in Excel 2007 (and higher) products on a PC for maximum functionality. The spreadsheets might work on earlier versions of Excel, but with possible changes in functionality and formatting. Google Docs, Openoffice.org, and other spreadsheet programs may or may not operate these spreadsheets correctly. For those Etsy-preneurship readers who do not have a spreadsheet system that will open these files, I have also provided printable downloadable PDF files. Every computer should be able to open PDF files using Adobe Reader (http://get.adobe.com/reader/).

For all downloads, I suggest you save an initial copy that you keep as a permanent copy and then save a second version of the file with a new filename for your working copy. I have left all formulas unprotected in these spreadsheets so you can customize them as you see fit. You do not need to know how to operate a spreadsheet program to use these tools. I have designed them in a way that, if you can navigate the web, you should be able to navigate the spreadsheets. At the end of each chapter, I will provide any special instructions or teachings related to that chapter's specific download.

Download: Mission, Vision, Values, and Competency Statements

The first step toward practicing Etsy-preneurship is to know the "why" behind your business. The "why" behind your business can be found in four statements: the mission statement, the vision statement, the values statement, and the competency statement. These four statements can sound a little stuffy, but I have found them to be very helpful to focus small business owners on what their business is really about. These four statements will help make up the first section of your business plan.

Mission Statement

A mission statement defines the purpose of your business. It is a high-level goal that provides context and guidance to help you make future business decisions. It shows the aims of your business. The mission statement is broad enough to grow with your business, wherever it might take you years from now. Mission statements are for both you and your customers to read. It tells a customer why you are in business and is a form of your business brand. A mission statement is a type of philosophy you can fall back on when you are uncertain about a direction your business is taking. Here are a couple examples of Etsy sellers' mission statements:

Coil and Flame designs and creates miniature pieces of art in jewelry form using sterling silver with mixed metals and gemstones. Each finished design is a one-of-a-kind or limited production piece that is a jewelry wardrobe investment for the discerning customer. Through online sales, home parties, and local networks, we maintain and attract customers with exceptional quality and service.

—Coil and Flame, by DLPom LLC

The purpose of my business is to share how I view the world through photography. Photography is a passion. With the advent of the digital age, I use my trained eye through the monitor of my digital camera, taking advantage of color saturations, macro close-ups, and the full range of editing. It is of utmost importance that any business transactions are for the customer. Whatever I can do to assure a positive experience for the customer is exactly what will happen.

—Lilleypics by Amy Lilley

Vision Statement

A vision statement is like looking into the future through a window you never looked out of before. What do you see? It provides inspiration to you by revealing your hopes and dreams for your business. It is bigger than a year in the future: It is what your business looks like 5 or 10 years from now. A vision statement should make you want to get out of bed in the morning and get right to work. Passion is poking itself into the vision statement. A vision statement is not typically seen by your customers, but is for your eyes only. Following are some examples of Etsy sellers' vision statements:

Coil and Flame's handmade jewelry business will be a recognized name in North America for modernly classic, sterling, and mixed metal jewelry designs. Visibility and demand of innovative jewelry designs will be increased through a presence in galleries and juried shows, ultimately growing the small business into a full-time venture.

—Coil and Flame, by DLPom LLC

My vision for my Etsy shop, Lilleypics is expansive. It is my hope to see my work, art, and photography broaden in depth and width over the next five years. Having just relocated to Colorado from New England, my inner and outer landscapes feel like they are being colored with a very, very broad brushstroke. Looking forward is easy, as every day is a new, awe-inspiring adventure for my eyes!

—Lilleypics, by Amy Lilley

Values Statement

A values statement defines what behaviors are important to you as you run your business. It defines your core traits. These core traits then help you represent your highest priorities. Your personal beliefs can also influence your values.

Your values will help you define how you spend your time and with what type of attitude.

My business values are *excellence, integrity*, and *service*. I value a lot of other traits, but these are the few I focus on. I believe that if you choose too many values, none of them will be evident in your business. Other popular business values include honesty, love, kindness, patience, humility, persistence, wisdom, courage, flexibility, optimism, fun, compassion, learning, generosity, dignity, respect, loyalty, innovation, customer service, creativity, discipline, communication, reliability, responsibility, quality, timeliness, orderliness, accuracy, and hundreds of others.

Competency Statement

A competency statement is a list of what you do well that makes your business distinct. These strengths can be things that set you and your business apart from other individuals and their businesses. These competencies are not always unique, but they are not easy to duplicate. Your competencies help your customers build additional trust in you, your products, and your business. Competencies can give your business a competitive advantage over other businesses.

Some of my business competencies include small business consultation, taxes, bookkeeping, customer service, and teaching. Other business competencies might include skills or strengths you have. Your competencies can include specific skills related to your craft, your eye for design, photography or literary abilities, or even business acumen.

Download Instructions

Note: To download this document, please go to www.etsy-preneurship.com/downloads.

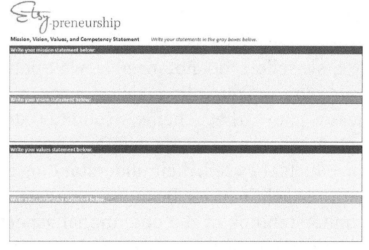

Access the download and write your four statements. These four statements will also serve as the first of five total parts of your business plan.

Chapter 2

Creating a Business Plan

A business plan is a written account of the who, what, where, when, why, and how of your business. Many successful Etsy sellers have gone through the process of creating a business plan. Small business owners create business plans in order to secure funding from banks or investors; this proves to the respective lending institutions that the business owners will make a profit and run a legitimate business.

Most Etsy sellers do not need a well-polished business plan. Instead, Etsy sellers need a basic business plan that helps solidify details highlighting their purposes, what their business is, what products they sell, their understanding of the market they sell in, their business strategies, and their understanding of the operational aspects of their business. A business plan is for your eyes only. The Etsy-preneurship business plan incorporates elements that are typically found in a business plan, but also includes elements that are found in some marketing plans. This plan is designed specifically with Etsy sellers in mind.

Business plans are not just for businesses that are starting out, but also for businesses that have been around for a while. I've read in the online Etsy forums of some Etsy sellers who had been selling for a few years that they put together their first business plan after their business had developed. After creating their business plans, these individuals learned something new about their products, business, and the market that they are a part of; this helped them with the future direction of their business. I suggest creating a business plan in the start-up phase of your business, but don't skip this step just because you might have already started your business. In fact, reviewing your business plan every year is a good exercise to see how things have changed or whether your business focus might be going in a slightly different direction than you originally planned.

Business plans are living documents. What you put down today will be valid for the moment, but even a few days later, parts of the plan might change. This is to be expected, because the environment in which you sell and run your business is in constant fluctuation. Don't worry about it! Also, don't worry about writing down things you are not 100 percent sure about. This is a plan, not a set-in-stone, never-to-be-changed, I-know-all-the-answers type of document. This is the beginning of a firm foundation for your business.

Starting the Foundation

All buildings that last have a firm foundation. The type of business I want to help you build is one that lasts, thrives, and is strong enough to withstand the challenges and oppositions that will eventually face it. A hut built on sand will fall when the wind and waves hit it, just like a business without a solid foundation will fall when competition increases or a large challenge surprises the business owner. In fact, if you have already completed the exercise in Chapter 1 (creating your mission, vision, values, and competency statements), you already have the first part of the foundation complete. These statements are the introduction to your business plan.

Benefits of Planning

Some of the benefits you will experience from creating your own business plan include:

- Understanding what your business is all about. No one in the world knows your business as well as you do, and if you don't know it well, there is no way you can expect your customer to know your business.
- Giving you greater clarity when setting goals for your business.
- Providing you with a point of reference when making difficult business decisions or when you need guidance.
- Giving you peace that although there are many moving parts and unknowns in starting and running a business, you are well prepared.
- Making you proactive to the challenges that face your business.
- Helping you quantify or measure what success will look like for your business. Defining success helps you know when you reach or get one step closer to it.
- Ensuring that your implementation is consistent with your mission, vision, values, and competencies.

- Providing you practical guidance toward financial funding and managing revenues, costs, and profits.
- Making you aware of the environment in which your business operates.
- Igniting you with motivation to achieve your plan.
- Assisting you in focusing on setting the priorities that will eventually be the tasks that make your business great!

Breaking Down the Business Plan

The Etsy-preneurship business plan focuses on four additional key areas: defining your product, analyzing your market, developing your strategy, and planning your operations. The fifth key area is defining your purpose (mission, vision, values, and competencies), which you already finalized at the end of Chapter 1. Let's start learning about the four new business plan topics before we create your Etsy shop's business plan in an exercise at the end of this chapter.

Defining Your Product

The product that you sell is the most important part of your business. If you have no product to sell on Etsy, you don't have a business. The varieties of products that are sold on Etsy are numerous. There are 31 categories of items for sale on Etsy: accessories, art, bags and purses, bath and beauty, books and zines, candles, ceramics and pottery, children, clothing, crochet, dolls and miniatures, everything else, furniture, geekery, glass, holidays, housewares, jewelry, knitting, music, needlecraft, paper goods, patterns, pets, plants and edibles, quilts, supplies, toys, vintage, weddings, and woodworking. In addition, these 31 categories are broken down into more than 500 subcategories!

Some of these categories are more crowded and have more competition than others. However, do not let the fact that there is a lot of competition deter you. Also, do not let this stop you from entering a market that has fewer sellers; it is merely something to be aware of when defining your product.

Imagine that Etsy is a large grocery store. It is important to realize where your products would be located within the store to understand your part in the larger Etsy environment. If there were 20 aisles in this grocery store, jewelry would make up four and a half aisles; vintage would make up almost three aisles; and supplies would make up nearly two and a half of the aisles. This means that almost half of the "Etsy store" consists of products made up of jewelry, vintage items, and supplies!

It is important to think about which categories your products will be sold under. Will you try to focus on one of these specific categories, or will you try to sell in many of these categories? Another option is to create one type of product that fits into many of the categories.

Etsy Inventory by Category

Category	Inventory	%	Category	Inventory	%	Category	Inventory	%
Jewelry	2,835,562	24.5%	Crochet	226,941	2.0%	Patterns	93,523	0.8%
Vintage	2,160,557	18.7%	Everything else	202,426	1.7%	Needlecraft	84,719	0.7%
Supplies	1,751,199	15.1%	Bath and beauty	150,417	1.3%	Toys	70,688	0.6%
Art	1,200,046	10.4%	Knitting	136,426	1.2%	Plants and edibles	57,190	0.5%
Accessories	855,970	7.4%	Glass	130,042	1.1%	Books and zines	56,942	0.5%
Children	709,191	6.1%	Ceramics and pottery	127,195	1.1%	Quilts	52,265	0.5%
Housewares	533,780	4.6%	Dolls and miniatures	119,111	1.0%	Candles	47,325	0.4%
Paper goods	516,916	4.5%	Geekery	112,515	1.0%	Furniture	28,348	0.2%
Clothing	419,008	3.6%	Pets	103,522	0.9%	Music	11,297	0.1%
Weddings	312,133	2.7%	Holidays	96,943	0.8%	Total inventory @ May 2012	11,584,073	100.0%
Bags and purses	289,711	2.5%	Woodworking	96,798	0.8%			

Etsy has standards about what type of products can be sold on the site. The three types of items that can be sold on Etsy are those handmade by you, crafting supplies, and vintage goods. Details outlining these three categories can be found on Etsy by visiting the help page and searching the phrase, "What items can I sell on Etsy?" I suggest you read these rules carefully, as you don't want to start or run a business that would eventually be shut down because you are breaking Etsy's rules. Clearly define your product by appearance, materials, and size.

Materials

What are the core materials you will use in making your products? Where will you get these materials? Where will you store them? What quantity of raw materials will you have on hand at any one point? Will you buy materials on a just-in-time basis to make a product, or will you have supplies already on hand? Do you foresee yourself becoming a raw material hoarder? If so, what will you do to stop this from causing too many expenses for your business? Will you buy materials from the major crafting supply companies or from smaller crafting suppliers? Do your materials stand out from other materials used on Etsy? Do your materials match your brand and image?

Quality

What standards of raw materials will you use? Will they be environmentally safe? Organic? Mass-produced? Are your materials safe to sell to others? Do your materials lend themselves to creativity? Is your end product of good quality, professional quality, or elite quality? Will that quality of product match your brand and target market of customers?

Pricing Philosophy

There are many things to consider when pricing individual products. We cover this in greater detail in Chapter 5, "Finances," but now is the time to start considering your pricing philosophy with regard to the materials you use, brand image you are creating, and target market. There is a psychology in pricing. Product prices ending in whole dollars are viewed as more upscale. Product prices ending fractions of a dollar are often viewed by customers as value items.

What will your Etsy business's price points be? Price points are the range of prices that are offered in your shop. A low price point might be an item for sale for a few dollars. Almost everyone can afford this item to "test out" your business at low risk to themselves. An average price point might be in the $15 to $40 range. High price point ranges will then be more expensive, with no limit in price. I believe it is important for Etsy sellers to include all three price ranges in their shops, because of the variety of people who shop on Etsy. One exception to this rule is if you are specifically targeting low- or high-income individuals or customers who have specific connections associated with a product and its related price. Your competitors' pricing, your material costs, and your profit margin desires should also be considered when creating your pricing philosophy.

Analyzing Your Market

The second key area in your business plan is gaining a better understanding of the market your Etsy shop will be a part of. Understanding your customers, your market (on and off of Etsy), and your competition (on and off of Etsy) will give you knowledge of how to best brand your business. All of this knowledge helps you develop your brand, which will give your business its identity.

Customer Need

Why should your customers buy your product? What need or want does it satisfy? What solution does it provide for them? In what circumstances would they purchase your product? Are they buying the product for themselves or as a gift? Are they buying it as a luxury or a necessity? Are they buying it as part of their regular budget or a splurge? Is it a planned purchase or an impulse buy? Do your customers have the option of buying this at a much lower price at a big-box retailer? Why would they purchase your product instead of making it themselves? Can your customer make your product themselves? Are they buying your product to save time? Are they buying your product because they heard about you from a friend? Are they trying to impress someone with your product? Are they buying your product because they have bought into your business brand? How fast do your customers expect to receive your products in the mail?

Customer needs help you define how your business will meet their needs and wants. Let their needs influence your product, brand, and business identity.

Customer Profile

What do your average customers look like? How old are they? How much money do they make a year? Are they repeat Etsy customers or brand new to Etsy? Are they male or female? Do they live in the country or city? What part of the world do they live in? What culture are they part of? What are their values? What are their professions? What are their hobbies? What websites do they visit? What does their social life look like? Are they married or single? What music do they listen to? What style or design do they like? What books, magazines, or newspapers do they read? What are their education levels? What social media sites do they use?

Customer profiles help you understand who you are selling to and how your brand matches their profile. Knowing your customer profile will also help you build intentional relationships with your customers through social media.

Market Trends

Your business is part of many markets. First, you are part of the global marketplace of products—this includes everything that is for sale in the world. Second, you are part of the Etsy marketplace. Third, you are part of specific categories or niches of products within Etsy. What has been happening in these markets recently? What type of products are popular sellers? What colors are hot? What price points are selling well?

Looking at market trends helps you determine where your business needs to go to meet or create its own trends. Trends change through time. As a business owner, you will have to decide how much trendsetting and trend following you will perform. Both methods have their advantages and require different marketing tactics.

Competitor Analysis

I enjoy competition and believe that competition makes businesses perform with excellence and at higher levels. Although Etsy is a very community-centric environment, it is still a capitalist environment, where limited money is purchasing a large variety and quantity of products. You want the demand for the supply of your products to be high. You can wish your competitors success as your business also succeeds.

I think it is important to look at possible direct competitors who are already selling on Etsy as well as your direct competitors who are selling off of Etsy. Direct competitor businesses that sell products very similar to yours. Indirect competitors sell products that are not acutely related to yours but that are related to your products. Here are some important things to learn from looking at your competitors:

- What are their strengths and weaknesses? Are there any opportunities or threats they face?
- What do they do well?
- What do they not do well, and how could you do better?
- What experience or experiences do you have that they don't have?
- Why would a customer choose your business over theirs?
- What is their pricing strategy?
- How does their product quality compare to your product quality?
- How would you describe their brand and image?
- What target market are they trying to fill?
- Do they advertise? How? Does it appear to be working?
- How are their social media connections? What is working well for them? Why?
- How long has their business been in operation?
- What can you learn from their business?

I suggest that you find small businesses that you admire that are completely unrelated to your business and ask the same questions. Looking at other businesses is a way to be inspired and learn from their mistakes.

Pure business copycats are oftentimes not successful, because they lack the spark of creativity. Watch out for the desire to imitate an Etsy shop that you regard highly. I suggest you find Etsy shops that embody qualities you appreciate, as they will inspire you to do better, but don't copy them. Find aspects from many Etsy shops that you like, then emulate those qualities in your own way. A business that operates with great innovation often fails, but a business that comes along afterward often makes some tweaks and does a better job. Let your competition motivate you to greatness. Wish them success. The market on Etsy is very large and there is room for many to succeed. If someone else eventually imitates you, feel flattered and keep on innovating! Business is not static.

Developing Your Strategy

The third key area in your business plan is developing and refining your business strategy. A business strategy is a plan of action to achieve your main objectives. Developing your strategy is an important step toward implementing your business. Tactics are something you do to achieve your strategies. Strategies come before tactics. The tactics of your business will be the operational activities you perform. Strategies do not change as often as tactics change. Strategies have a longer-term focus.

Niche

A niche is a small part of the market in which you will seek to operate, influence, and succeed. A niche needs to be narrow enough that you can influence it, but wide enough that you have enough customers. If your niche is selling "anklet charms for left-handed individuals who live in France and enjoy soccer and only work part-time," your niche might be too small. There is no magical way of knowing whether a niche is the perfect fit for your business; it is about trusting your business instincts and evaluating the results of your business. Niches can change if they are not working out, but if you find a niche that works, stick with it! Use all your market analysis to help define what your business niche is. My niche is this: "Etsy sellers who want to improve their business." My wife's Etsy shop's niche: "Moms who like Amy Butler fabric and like having stylish babies." Clearly define your niche.

Keys to Success

Every business faces some key hurdles or challenges to overcome. These keys to success are constantly evolving. What do you think those keys to success are for your business right now? If you can't list out your keys to success, the chances of you succeeding are reduced drastically, because your direction lacks focus. Examples of keys to success include designing a brand, logo, and name that will last many years; learning how to market on Facebook and manage your brand, and creating a spending plan so you don't go into too much debt before you start to make a profit. Everyone's keys to success are different based on skill levels and even personal weaknesses. Identifying what you think will help you succeed is a great exercise in refining your strategies.

Branding Strategy

What is your business's name? Does anyone else have that name or a similar name? Is the domain (dot-com) of that name available? (Domain registration service links are available on Etsy-preneurship.com.) What is your business's tagline? What is the personality of your business? If your business had a commercial, what would the commercial say? What color scheme matches your business? How will you use those color schemes? What is the tone you communicate and relate to your customers and fans via social media? Do your mission, vision, values, and competencies match your brand?

When you build a business, you are also building a brand. The two are inseparable. Spend a good amount of time naming your business and its tagline. You don't want to have to change the name of your business at a later date. Etsy currently allows you to change your shop's name once, but it is much better to get it correct the first time!

Planning Your Operations

The last area of your business plan helps to refine your strategies and start considering specific tactics and big-picture operational considerations. This is the beginning of what will eventually become your business's operational standards (the subject of Chapter 7).

Funding

How will you fund the start-up or operations of your business? Will you go into debt to achieve this? What levels of debt are acceptable? What will your initial profits be used for (growing and expanding your business or withdrawing them for personal use)? Do you have a limit on how much money your business could lose before you call it quits? Will you fund your business operations from your business revenues only or from personal funds? Setting some financial goals and targets or budgets will also be important for your business. We cover these topics in more detail in Chapter 5.

Suppliers

Where will you buy your supplies? Will you be able to avoid paying sales tax on the materials you purchase by having a state sales tax ID? How often will you buy supplies?

Revenue Streams

Will you sell your products in venues other than Etsy? On other websites? In boutiques? At craft shows or home shows? Or anywhere else you can think of? There are many sellers on Etsy who sell only on Etsy, but many Etsy sellers eventually branch out into other selling venues. One benefit of diversifying your revenue streams is that all your revenue eggs are not in one basket. All businesses have to start selling somewhere, and I think Etsy is the best place to start. Over time, I do suggest all

Etsy sellers diversify their selling venues to lower the risks of counting on revenue from only one source.

SMART Goals

What goals do you want to set for your business right now? Goals should be SMART: Specific, Measurable, Attainable, Realistic, and Timely. Specific goals answer the who, what, when, where, why, and how questions related to a goal. The measurable aspect of a goal should have something that can be tracked. If you can't track a goal, you will never know if you achieve it. An attainable goal is one that you can influence to come true. It is within your reach. The goal should also be realistic. Don't shoot for making 100,000 sales in a month if you are currently making only 10 sales a month. Last, a goal should be timely. Put a time element on all goals so you know the point by which you must achieve the goal. This helps light the fire and motivate you to make progress on the goals in incremental steps.

Depending on what stage your business is in right now will influence what type of goals you have. I constantly have goals for my business and know that businesses that are growing and thriving always have evolving goals. I suggest you make five big goals. Underneath each goal, write out the tasks that you will have to accomplish to achieve that particular goal. Goals broken down into smaller pieces are easier to achieve. Try to initially set goals that can be achieved within three months. Three months gives you time to achieve some larger goals, but are not so long a time period that your goals are lost or lose momentum.

Planning Calendar

Once you have your specific goals and the tasks related to these goals, it is time to make a plan to implement these into reality. I suggest you plan out your three months week by week. This gives you daily flexibility to pick and choose what you work on, yet enough accountability to keep you on track and not falling behind. Not everyone works well with such a detailed plan, so use your knowledge about yourself to plan accordingly. Maximizing your effectiveness in scheduling will serve you well as your business grows and matures. Managing, planning, and scheduling your time is a valuable skill that can be learned with practice.

Download: Creating Your Etsy Business Plan

Note: To download this document, please go to <u>www.etsy-preneurship.com/downloads</u>.

Using this business plan tool will walk you through all the applicable parts to create your unique Etsy-preneurship business plan. After answering all the questions in the tool, you will have details regarding defining your purpose, defining your product, analyzing your market, developing your strategy, and planning your operations. Save a copy of this document to review periodically and modify as your market and environment change.

Chapter 3

Bookkeeping

Bookkeeping is the task of keeping the financial records for your business. Typical bookkeeping systems include paper and pencil, spreadsheet, software, or an online-based system. Bookkeeping allows you to make better business decisions and file necessary taxes. Bookkeeping is one of the key administrative tasks that many Etsy sellers struggle with in terms of knowing when and where to start; this trepidation is usually a result of their having little to no experience with it. Every Etsy seller will need to find a bookkeeping system that meets his or her respective needs. The best bookkeeping system for you is the one that you will use consistently and comfortably. The best time to start bookkeeping for your small business is now.

I know of Etsy sellers who get a bookkeeping system ready to use before they make their first sale or generate their first expense. These sellers are better prepared for the bookkeeping responsibilities facing their business. I also know of Etsy sellers who have started their bookkeeping three years into selling on Etsy. These free spirits are stressed out because they have to re-create three years of financial activities all at once; this is extremely difficult (but not impossible), not to even mention the tax nightmare this creates.

Benefits of Bookkeeping

There are both proactive and reactive reasons for performing bookkeeping for your small business. Proactive reasons include making better financial decisions, avoiding financial mistakes, and tracking the financial success of your business. The reactive reason for performing bookkeeping, for most Etsy sellers, is that it is required for filing taxes. Many Etsy sellers view bookkeeping only as a necessary evil, which it is, but I suggest a more holistic view of bookkeeping: Because bookkeeping is necessary for your small business, you should make it as fun and simple as possible. The following guidelines will help you do so:

- *Ease in filing taxes.* Most Etsy sellers are sole proprietors (i.e., work for themselves and own their own business) and, if they do business in the United States, file Schedule C each year at tax time. It is impossible to file Schedule C unless you keep your books throughout the year. A few Etsy sellers perform bookkeeping only once a year, and this means they are potentially harming themselves and their business. They are most likely missing transactions and not taking advantage of the proactive benefits of bookkeeping. Most Etsy sellers do not create all their products at one time during the year and then sell them throughout the year. In the same way, Etsy sellers should not save all their bookkeeping tasks for tax time.

- *Making better decisions.* When you perform bookkeeping throughout the year, you see your financial results as they happen. You have time to adjust things if you don't like the results. Seeing your results will also help you forecast or get an idea of where your finances will be at the end of the year. You will be able to spot trends in inventory, sales, expenses, and raw materials that might make you adjust your operations. Many Etsy sellers will need to make quarterly financial tax payments, and bookkeeping will help determine how much to pay.

- *Avoiding financial mistakes.* I know of too many Etsy shops that have failed or struggled because they overspent on raw materials without being able to sell the products. They essentially made their business go bankrupt by putting too much cash into the business without returns in sales. Financial mistakes cause businesses to fail or put them back years in progress. Having order and structure in your business finances is one of the smartest foundations for long-term business success.

- *Tracking your success.* When you start making money selling on Etsy, it is fun to watch the progress your business is making in sales and profit. Seeing trends and graphs moving upward is encouraging and helps motivate you to continue improving your business. Knowing how much profit you make will also help you make decisions about whether to reinvest profits back into your business or take the money out of your business accounts and transfer them to a personal account.

Talking the Bookkeeping Talk

Like most skills, bookkeeping has its own language and specific meanings for words. Let's take a look at some of the key definitions.

- *Revenue.* Revenue is all the money you receive from customers. It includes any money they pay you for your product, including sales tax and shipping fees. The gross amount is recorded. This amount does not include any money taken out for PayPal or Etsy fees.
- *Expenses.* Expenses are anything you spend money on to run your business. The expense must be necessary and ordinary for tax purposes. (Don't try to expense a trip to Paris for a family vacation!) Cost of goods sold is a type of expense.
- *Cost of goods sold (COGS).* The cost of the materials used to make one product is the cost of the goods. When the item sells, it becomes a cost of goods sold. COGS will

be covered in greater detail in Chapter 4, "Taxes."

- *Profit.* Revenues minus expenses equals profit. Profit is what you are taxed on. Profit is one reason why you are in business. Businesses have the intent to make a profit.
- *Raw material.* Raw materials are the items or things used by you to make the finished products you hope to sell. Raw materials eventually become finished inventory.
- *Finished inventory.* Finished inventory is made up of raw materials ready to sell. Finished inventory eventually becomes sold inventory and revenue.
- *Transaction.* A transaction is a financial event that requires some form of bookkeeping to take place. Examples of transactions include a sale and a purchase. Other types of transactions can relate to raw materials and inventory (buying materials, making a product, and selling a product).
- *Cash basis accounting.* Most Etsy sellers use the cash basis of accounting, meaning

that if there is a change in cash, there is a bookkeeping transaction that takes place. The cash basis of accounting always follows the cash. Keeping good records of cash is a simple way to make sure your bookkeeping is accurate. The alternative to cash basis accounting is *accrual accounting*. Accrual accounting recognizes an economic event even if cash does not change hands. Larger businesses typically use the accrual method of accounting.

Core Bookkeeping Functionality

Various bookkeeping systems offer different functionality. The following are what I consider to be the minimum requirements when looking for a bookkeeping system for your business. Other bells and whistles may make your life easier and are great and useful, but not essential to bookkeeping.

Sales Tracking

Every Etsy seller will make sales, and it is necessary to keep track of these. At a bare minimum, you should track the sale amount, the date of the sale, what you sold, and the name of the customer. If you receive all your sales through PayPal, you can download all your sales in a *comma-separated values* (CSV) file, which can be opened using a spreadsheet. If all your sales are on Etsy, you can also download a sales CSV file by month (found in Your Shop, Options, Download Data, and Orders). If you make sales in places other than Etsy, it is crucial to track these as well. This will help ensure that you, your business, and your financial health remain strong and accurate for tax reporting purposes.

Expense Tracking

If you pay for something to help run your business, you should track it. Tracking all business-related expense reduces your net profit, which means you have less taxable profit. And this means more money for you in the long run. At a minimum, track the date you made the purchase, what you bought, and the amount of the expense.

Raw Material Tracking

Most Etsy sellers have raw materials sitting around waiting to be made into finished products. Tracking raw materials when you purchase them and then when you use them in a product helps you know what the true raw material cost of a product is. You can use this knowledge when you are creating the price of your product. If you never track these costs, you could be selling your items for less than the cost of the raw materials. This is a surefire way to go out of business quickly. Typical raw material details to track include the name or description of the item, how much each item costs, how many you originally purchased, how many were used, and how many are remaining. Typical units of measurement include count, weight, volume, length, yardage, and other measurements.

Finished Inventory Tracking

When those raw materials turn into a finished product, it is important to track the finished inventory you have on hand. It is specifically important to note your finished inventory values at the beginning and end of each year, in case you need that information for tax purposes. Typical finished inventory details to track include what the item is, how many you have, how many you have sold, how many are remaining, the product's retail sales price, and the related raw material costs associated with that product.

Tracking your finished inventory levels is very telling and useful. Doing so, for example, could help you build up finished inventory for a big sale or craft show. It could also indicate that you may be building up too much finished inventory. If so, you would know to focus more time on selling some of what you have rather than on continuing to make new products.

Cash Management

Since most Etsy sellers are on a cash basis of accounting, tracking cash makes a lot of sense. You should be able to see a direct relationship between your cash transactions and your bookkeeping entries. If you watch your PayPal and business-only bank account carefully, you will be able to ensure that all of your transactions are being recorded. It is also helpful to keep tabs on how much cash your business has on hand at any one time. Not having cash when you need it is very hurtful—it can either cause you to close your business or miss out on good business opportunities. I suggest you track your balances, the inflows and outflows of cash, as well as the date of the flows and their description. It is also helpful to watch how cash balances increase and decrease through a series of months.

Reporting

Bookkeeping will serve its purpose only if you remain focused on the big picture. Imagine hundreds of lines of details on transactions and inventory. When you look at hundreds of little pieces of details and numbers, it is hard to interpret which information is useful for you. That is why all bookkeeping systems should have some form of reporting. It can be as simple as a summary of all monthly sales, expenses, and inventory levels or as fancy as customizable graphs to show you everything you could ever possibly want to see relating to the finances of your business.

Typical Bell-and-Whistle Features

Some bookkeeping systems include some nonfinancial information to track along with your finances, including marketing data; business-related mileage for the IRS; social media statistics, contact information; bill trackers, sales tax trackers; and cash/bank/PayPal account tracking. If you are more of visual person, you may want to also consider the type of graphs and reports that are created automatically.

Most Popular Etsy Bookkeeping Solutions

There is no one right or wrong solution to performing your business's bookkeeping. In fact, you could even do your bookkeeping on napkins, carved in stone, or a painted canvas! Here we explore the most commonly used bookkeeping solutions that Etsy sellers are employing. I also point out some of the advantages and disadvantages each solution offers.

Paper and Pencil

Paper-and-pencil solutions typically use premade bookkeeping templates or forms. They may include a general bookkeeping ledger (to track sales and expenses), a finished inventory tracker, summary reports, and other practical forms. This method is often the least expensive to begin implementing. Forms are printed out and usually put in a binder. Sellers with lower volumes of sales and expenses often use this type of solution. Prices are typically around $30 to $50.

Advantages: These systems are simple to use, have low start-up costs, are always right there on your desk, and track only the bare minimum. They require no technical expertise; you can customize tracking by adding a column to a form; you own the bookkeeping solution; and they are often designed with only Etsy sellers in mind.

Disadvantages: They require manual entries by hand and use a lot of paper. You have to use a calculator to create summary reports; they are more susceptible to math errors; and the solution does not grow with your business's growth.

Spreadsheet

Spreadsheet bookkeeping solutions are typically made using Microsoft Excel or a similar word processor application. Spreadsheets can be customizable to track almost anything on a whim. They typically have multiple tabs or sections where transactions are recorded, and they can perform the math for you. To take it even a step further, they can even generate graphs and reports automatically after you enter transactions.

Although spreadsheets have the ability to track only the bare-minimum requirements, they are also able to track many other variables. If your business uses a variety of different types of raw materials, and you are concerned with tracking your COGS for tax and pricing purposes, a spreadsheet is often the best solution. Most spreadsheet bookkeeping systems are designed so you can use them even if you have never used a spreadsheet before. Prices are typically around $60 to $100.

Advantages: These systems are fully customizable to track anything you want; reports and graphs update automatically; they include COGS tracking; colors can be customized to your brand's colors;

they may be used year after year; they provide a lower-cost solution; they are electronic, easy to back up and save, contain no math errors, and are designed with Etsy sellers in mind; you can copy and paste data from PayPal and Etsy CSV files; and you own the bookkeeping solution.

Disadvantages: Formulas can be overwritten, and you have to open the file every time you use it.

Software

There are many types of bookkeeping software solutions to choose from; you simply purchase the software you want and install it on your computer. From my experience, the software-based bookkeeping system most widely used by Etsy sellers is QuickBooks. QuickBooks is a bookkeeping solution that is typically used by businesses that are larger than Etsy sellers. QuickBooks allows you to create invoices, print checks, and manage bills. Through the Etsy forums and in conversations with many Etsy sellers, I've seen that some Etsy sellers are very satisfied with QuickBooks, but more typically I hear from Etsy sellers who are not satisfied with it because it does not handle COGS easily, has functions they never use, and is not particularly easy to learn. Prices range from $185 to $200.

Advantages: Reports are generated automatically; functionality works even when your business begins to hire employees. You can send invoices to customers, print checks, and avoid math errors, and you own the bookkeeping solution.

Disadvantages: QuickBooks is more costly than other solutions; there's very little customization; you have to learn the software features; and the system is built for larger business functionality.

Online

There has been a recent growth in online bookkeeping solutions offered for small business owners. The most talked-about online solution for Etsy sellers is Outright.com. Outright integrates with your PayPal account, Etsy account, eBay account, and many bank and credit card companies to import your financial information into its bookkeeping solution. Outright offers a free account with limited functionality, as well as a more robust account for $9.95 per month. The feedback I hear in the forums from the Etsy community is mixed. The Etsy sellers who love it typically cite the automation. The Etsy sellers who don't like it cite technical issues, errors, security, and the monthly charge. Also, QuickBooks now has an online solution that can be found at QuickBooks.com.

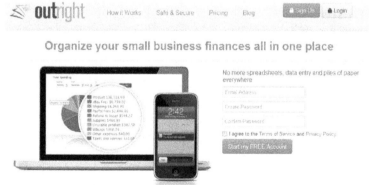

Advantages: You have online access; there's no paper, no monthly fee for sales tax reporting and quarterly tax tracking, and no manual entries.

Disadvantages: There is a monthly fee for some features, no customization, no COGS tracking, and systems are designed for general online sellers (not Etsy-specific). In addition, the provider has access to your financial data (security concerns), and you don't own the bookkeeping solution. Once you start using a bookkeeping solution such as Outright, it is difficult to stop using the service, because all your data is in its system and cannot be exported to be used in a different system.

My Bookkeeping Recommendations

All four solutions perform bookkeeping very well and will meet your needs. Therefore, I can confidently say that you won't go wrong with any of them. Knowing Etsy sellers and having helped thousands of them perform their bookkeeping over the years, I think spreadsheets are the best solutions. For those who want to keep their bookkeeping really simple and don't care for all the customization, automatic reports, and graphs, I suggest a paper-and-pencil solution. I also suggest these methods because they are very reasonably priced and put Etsy shop owners in complete control of their bookkeeping.

Although I stand firm in my belief that all four solutions are viable, I do have some minor concerns with the current online solutions. My biggest concern with Outright is its access to your financial details if you use its monthly subscription solution—and it is too highly priced to use long term. Also, your business's bookkeeping is of utmost importance for filing your taxes. You are the only person in the world responsible for your taxes. Therefore, I like to be in control of the bookkeeping system that houses this information, and I especially don't want to risk it being lost or hacked into. My biggest concern with QuickBooks is that it is overkill for Etsy sellers—has functionality that is never used, requires a steeper learning curve, and is so broadly designed for all types of small businesses that some functionality is completely irrelevant or adds confusion.

In the interest of full disclosure, I have created multiple spreadsheet and paper-and-pencil–based Etsy-specific bookkeeping systems through the years. I have tried to not let my recommendations be influenced by this, but rather have tried to recommend systems to you in a professional manner, clearly stating the benefits and disadvantages of each system. At the end of the day, I believe spreadsheets and paper-and-pencil solutions are the most appropriate for Etsy sellers' bookkeeping needs. Remember, the best bookkeeping system is the one you will use consistently and don't mind using. Choose the solution that you will use consistently and that is most convenient for you.

Key Bookkeeping Topics and Tips

A variety of bookkeeping-related topics are of specific interest to Etsy sellers. Some of these topics include how to account for shipping fees, how to account for PayPal and Etsy transaction fees, how to keep up with receipts, tracking sales taxes, understanding bookkeeping cycles in your business, how to get your bookkeeping started, how to account for raw material waste or breakage, and practical bookkeeping tips that I have developed over the years that can make your bookkeeping go much smoother.

Shipping Fees

Shipping fees impact your business as both a revenue and expense activity. Revenue activity-related shipping fees are part of your total revenue received. If you sell a product for $15 and the customer also pays you $5 to ship the product, the customer pays you a total of $20. The entire $20 is revenue. You then expense the $5 shipping fee.

You also pay shipping fees when you order supplies or raw materials. You purchase raw materials for $35 and pay $8 for shipping them to your house. You pay a total of $43. The entire $43 is expensed and goes into your raw material tracker at $43. This $43 can then be used in determining your raw material costs of a product you made and impact your COGS.

PayPal and Etsy Fees

I suggest you record your Etsy fees only once a month as an expense line item in your bookkeeping solution. If you do this once a month when the Etsy bill becomes due, you will always have one transaction per month. I have heard of some Etsy sellers tracking their Etsy fees by item (even tracking how many times each item has been renewed). It does not hurt anything, but I believe this is overkill and does not provide much valuable financial information for decisions or tax purposes.

I also suggest you record your PayPal fees once a month as an expense line item in your bookkeeping solution. I typically download the CSV file from PayPal and open it in a spreadsheet. I highlight all the fees to see what the total PayPal fee was for the month. If you received a sale for $10 and the PayPal fee was $1, you would record the $10 as revenue and the $1 as an expense.

Receipts

Do not throw all your receipts into a shoebox for the year and then look at them when it comes time to file your taxes! Also, do not throw all your receipts into a shoebox and bring them to your accountant! Accountants simultaneously hate and like people who do this. Accountants hate this because they don't enjoy flipping through tiny pieces of paper and trying to decipher your financial story. They like it because they can charge you a lot more per hour and for more hours of work. Bottom line: Managing your receipts will save you a lot of time and a lot of money.

Receipts come in paper format, electronic format, or as downloadable CSV files. You can either print them all out and have a paper copy or scan them all into your computer to have all electronic copies. Most people use a mixture of both. The important thing is that you organize your receipts in some manner.

You can organize your receipts either in electronic file folders or in physical folders. You can organize them by month or by category of transaction. I prefer organizing by month, because it gives some chronological order to my financial transactions and can coincide with the monthly bookkeeping cycle I perform for my business. One issue to keep in mind when organizing receipts by category is that one receipt might have multiple categories on it. For example, you go to the craft store and buy fabric and envelopes. The fabric would be a raw material expense, but the envelope would fall into the administration or office supply category. In this case, you might need to make copies of the receipt, which is not the end of the world, but it can be a hassle.

I suggest you make all your business and personal transactions separately. When you go to the craft store and you buy something for your business, pay for that in one transaction. Then, have the cashier total up your personal purchases with a separate transaction and receipt. If you do happen to make a purchase and have a receipt that has both personal and business expenses on it, circle the business expenses right away, because you might not remember or be able to interpret the receipt when it is time to perform bookkeeping. If you think you might forget what a purchase was for, write it down on the receipt.

Make sure you save your receipts for several years. The IRS can come back and audit you for prior years. Receipts are the proof that a transaction took place, and you will need these to prove that the transaction took place and was for business purposes.

Tracking Sales Tax

Your bookkeeping is impacted by sales taxes on both the revenue and expense side of a transaction. On the revenue side, you might collect sales tax from a customer. The item sells for $10 and you also collect $1 for sales tax. The customer pays you a total of $11. You would book revenue of $11 and a payable (expense) of $1. Some states might treat the sales tax you collect as a liability where you pass the funds on to the state.

When you purchase raw materials, you might pay sales tax as part of that transaction. For example, you buy $40 of raw materials and the retailer charges you $4 of sales tax. You pay a total of $44. This $44 is all expensed.

Cycles

Bookkeeping is all about cycles. The most common financial cycles that face your business are monthly and annual cycles. Each month, you have bills that are most likely due. Annually, you have to file taxes for the calendar year. I suggest all Etsy sellers perform their bookkeeping monthly. Some Etsy sellers can get by doing it quarterly, but then they miss out on some of the insights of performing it monthly.

For the past seven years, I have used a monthly financial cycle for both personal and business finances and am very pleased with the results. Every first day of the month, I sit down for two hours and pay all my personal bills, write checks if necessary, and update my personal financial spreadsheet. Then, I perform all the bookkeeping for my small businesses for the month.

Benefits of performing bookkeeping once every month include:

- *Consistency.* When you do the same thing every single month, it becomes routine and you become more efficient at the task.
- *Comparability.* If you always perform your bookkeeping each month, it is easy to compare one month to another month. You will begin to be able to spot seasonality in your business and see which months are better or slower for your business.
- *Common cycle times.* Etsy charges you monthly, and you most likely have other bills related to your business that are charged in this same time period. Use this to your advantage to help you remember all of your transactions. Also, bank statements are typically reported monthly and can aid in helping you remember to record all your transactions.
- *Practicality.* Remembering what happened one month ago is reasonable.

Remembering what happened six months ago or one year ago is difficult.

I am aware of some Etsy sellers who update their bookkeeping in real time or daily, immediately when they make a sale or incur an expense. This is acceptable and will work. I do not recommend it because it can be distracting for your core business. Bookkeeping is a supporting part of your business, not what your business is all about. It would be more appropriate to check up on your bookkeeping in the middle of the month, or perhaps weekly, to see whether things seem to be on track financially.

Getting Started

If you are not currently performing any bookkeeping for your business, the best time to start is now. If you are starting to perform your bookkeeping after your business has been in operation for a while, you will need to re-create the bookkeeping for those prior months. The IRS does not give you a free pass just because you forgot or didn't want to perform your bookkeeping. In this case, find all the documentation or receipts that you can. Re-creating your revenue will probably be easier than re-creating your expenses, so you should easily be able to include all your revenue. For expenses, record only those expenses that you have a receipt for to prove the transaction took place.

If you have your bookkeeping system in place before you fully start your business or shortly after you start your business, you are in the perfect position to have an easy bookkeeping start-up.

Accounting for Waste, Scrap, and Freebies

When you are creating a finished product, you will most likely create some scrap or waste products. These are considered expense items when running a business. Any small, free products you give away are really advertising expenses in hopes of making future sales.

Practical Bookkeeping Tips

- Make bookkeeping as fun as possible. Turn on music. Customize your spreadsheet to your business colors. Treat yourself to chocolate when you are finished!
- Find someone to hold you accountable for performing your bookkeeping. Tell a

friend or family member how much you made in sales or profit each month. They will begin to expect to hear from you each month.

- Do your bookkeeping on the same day of the month around the same time to help with consistency.
- Block out a set amount of time when you will not be interrupted.
- Use the task of bookkeeping to improve your attention to detail. As an artist, attention to detail can improve your craft.

Download: Bookkeeping Quiz—Finding Your Solution

Note: To download this document, please go to www.etsy-preneurship.com/downloads.

 -preneurship

Bookkeeping Quiz—Finding Your Solution

1	I like the idea of making manual entries by hand.
2	I prefer only the simplest bookkeeping solution.
3	I prefer the absolute lowest-cost bookkeeping solution.
4	I have a low volume of sales and anticipate staying a low-volume seller.
5	I prefer not having to learn a new technical system.
6	I prefer seeing visual representation of my finances (graphs and charts).
7	I prefer the ability to customize bookkeeping to meet my needs (colors and data tracked).
8	I prefer all math calculations to happen automatically.
9	I prefer a system that can be accessed on the computer.
10	I prefer to own the bookkeeping solution and data it produces.
11	I prefer the ability to track raw materials and finished inventory.
12	I prefer giving the bookkeeping system access to my bank account, credit cards, and PayPal account to update automatically.
13	I prefer the ability to track my cash balances.
14	I dislike killing any trees.
15	I dislike using a calculator.
16	I prefer a bookkeeping system that can be used even after seven years of growth in my business.
17	I prefer a bookkeeping system that was designed specifically with only Etsy seller's needs in mind.
18	I prefer the ability to track social media and marketing information along with my bookkeeping data.
19	I prefer paying a one-time charge to acquire a bookkeeping solution.
20	I prefer paying a monthly fee to have access to a bookkeeping solution.
21	I prefer the ability to track cost of goods sold (COGS) easily for setting prices of my products.
22	I prefer a system that allows me to copy and paste financial data from PayPal and Etsy.
23	I prefer a system that is ready at a moment's notice—sitting on my desk.
24	I prefer a system I have to open a file or open a program.
25	I prefer a system that I can access on any computer, anytime, online.
26	I need to print invoices and check and have employer-related expenses.
27	I prefer the ability to transfer the data from my bookkeeping solution to another system, if needed.
28	I am greatly concerned about the security of my financial information.

Scroll down to see your results. Don't cheat! Answer all the questions before proceeding.

Taking this quiz will help you get an initial idea of what type of bookkeeping solution you might prefer; however, before committing to one type, make sure to research all four systems to find which type you believe you should use.

Chapter 4

Taxes

Taxes are one the most intimidating topics that Etsy sellers must become familiar with as small business owners, but don't sweat it! I have many Etsy tax seasons under my belt, and I know what you need to know to tame the tax monster. Almost all of the Etsy sellers that I have ever talked to want to pay their taxes, run a legal business, and not fear an IRS audit. The problem lies in the tax code: It is huge, uses difficult language, and is somewhat confusing. I will try to put it into everyday language and digestible-sized portions. Understanding the tax regulations that apply to your business takes time. I work with the tax code quite often and still learn something new almost every day!

Many Etsy sellers say, "I don't need to know the tax law. I'll just hire a tax expert to file my taxes." While I believe this is acceptable for some Etsy sellers with more complicated taxable situations, I do not promote that sentiment at all. First, I believe that the majority of Etsy sellers can file their own taxes, given the right knowledge and tools (which I will provide to you in this chapter). Second, even if you do end up hiring someone to file your taxes for you, there are many risks and detriments to not knowing the information that is in this chapter. As a sole proprietor, you are the person with ultimate responsibility for your taxes. If you have a tax-related error, it ultimately is your error. A strong foundation in basics of small business tax law gives you confidence that you are running a legal business and have nothing to fear from an IRS audit.

Tax Prerequisite

Etsy is a global marketplace, and the tax regulations around the world differ from each other. This chapter is written for US taxpayers who are sole proprietors of their business. If you live in a country other than the United States, I am providing the names of some agencies to help you get started in understanding your country's taxable responsibilities. If needed, consult your accountant regarding your specific taxable situations and requirements. Following is a list of some of the countries Etsy sellers reside in, along with the applicable agency to begin your research.

- United States: Internal Revenue Service (IRS)
- Canada: Canada Revenue Agency (CRA)
- European Union: EU member state Value Added Tax (VAT) regulations
- United Kingdom: Her Majesty's Revenue and Customs (HMRC)
- Australia: Australian Taxation Office (ATO)
- Japan: National Tax Agency
- Czech Republic: Ministry of Finance of the Czech Republic
- Denmark: Danish Ministry of Taxation (DMT)
- Hong Kong: Inland Revenue Ordinance (IRO)
- New Zealand: Inland Revenue Department (IRD)
- Norway: Norwegian Tax Administration
- Singapore: Inland Revenue Authority of Singapore
- Sweden: Swedish Tax Agency
- Switzerland: Swiss Federal Tax Administration

Some common questions to consider when researching the tax laws in your country include the following:

- Does your country have an income tax?
- What national tax laws will your business encounter?
- What local tax laws will your business need to follow?
- Does your country have a sales, use, or VAT-type tax on purchases and sales?
- How often will you have to pay your taxes, and to what agency?
- What forms will you have to complete, and how can you submit them?

Some good places to start your research are on the tax agency websites, personal blogs, and local and national newspaper articles. You can also look for an expert in your country's tax law, or seek out an experienced small business owner in your country for advice. The Etsy community might be another place you can find out more about your specific taxable requirements.

Do I Need to File Taxes?

Almost every day, I receive a convo (short for "conversations," Etsy's messaging system) on Etsy that in some roundabout way asks this question, and my answer is almost always yes. Unfortunately, this question is also often asked in Etsy forums, often drawing well-intentioned but ill-informed answers from various people, "No, it is just a hobby." "No, if you make under $___ [insert random number here] a year." "No, the IRS doesn't care about your shop. You're too small." "No, I don't know where to begin." "No, because my friend [spouse, other Etsy seller] told me I didn't have to." And hundreds of other answers containing the words *sometimes, maybe, yes, no,* and *probably.*

Stop and answer this question: "Do you want to make profit selling on Etsy?" *Stop*! Answer that question honestly.

The answer for 99.9 percent of people selling on Etsy is a loud, resounding *yes*! The reason most people want to make money on Etsy is because it sounds nice to have a fatter purse to pay off personal bills, save for a vacation, or meet another financial goal. Plus, there are great opportunities to make some profit! If you answer yes to this question, you have the intent to make a profit. This is also known as a business. A business has taxable obligations the moment it starts attempting to make a profit. There is no threshold required in sales or profits needed in order to be considered a business. The moment you make your first sale, you may have sales taxes that need to be collected. The moment you make your first sale, you have revenue reportable to the IRS on Schedule C as a sole proprietor. After a few sales, most Etsy sellers will have self-employment taxes due. The moment you start spending money in hopes of making money, you have expenses that need to be recorded on Schedule C to reduce your taxable income. You are a business in the eyes of the IRS and therefore have taxable responsibilities.

But wait, maybe you did not answer with a resounding *yes* to the question, "Do you want to make money selling on Etsy?" Instead, perhaps you answered, "This is just my hobby. Little ol' me, I'm too small to be a business. I certainly don't feel like one." Maybe you answered, "I'll just lose money on Etsy." Or maybe you sell on Etsy to fund the purchase of your own craft supplies. Let's look at how the IRS defines the differences between a hobby and a business.

Am I a Hobby or a Business?

The IRS has posted eight questions for individuals to answer to help determine whether they are a hobby or a business. Here are the questions, followed by my commentary.

1. Does the time and effort put into the activity indicate an intention to make a profit? If someone were to look at how much time you spent on your activities and making your products, would they consider it a full-time or part-time job? It does not take many hours to run a business. Previously, I have run a business by working only one hour during the month (not much happened, but it was still a business). Investing significant time signals that it is a business.

2. Does the taxpayer depend on income from the activity? If you are using the money, or if you have hopes of spending the money, from the proceeds of the activity, you most likely have a business in the eyes of the IRS.

3. If there are losses, are they due to circumstances beyond the taxpayer's control, or did they occur in the start-up phase of the business? When most businesses start up, they lose some money. If you are losing money as you start this activity, it might indicate to the IRS that you are trying to start a business.

4. *Has the taxpayer changed methods of operation to improve profitability?* The fact that you are reading this book probably means that you are, or will be, running a business. Actions taken to improve the chances of making more profits in your operations tell the IRS that you are a business.

5. *Does the taxpayer or his or her advisors have the knowledge needed to carry on the activity as a successful business?* If you have read books, visited websites to help you sell on Etsy, or have advisors who can help you carry on your activity, the IRS sees these as clues that you are a business.

6. *Has the taxpayer made a profit on similar activities in the past?* If you make profits, even if you believe your business to be a hobby, the IRS might believe this to be a business.

7. *Does the activity make a profit in some years?* If you make a profit some years and incur a loss other years, the IRS believes this points to a business.

8. *Can the taxpayer expect to make a profit in the future from the appreciation of assets used in the activity?* If you incur a large loss in one year (in the start-up phase) that the IRS believes will eventually turn into a profit, the IRS sees this as signs of a business.

If activities are indeed hobbies, losses from those activities may not be used to offset other income. According to the IRS, "Deductions for hobby activities are claimed as itemized deductions on Schedule A." The profits you make from your so-called hobby are taxable. When you have a hobby, you have limits to what you can expense to reduce that taxable income. As a business, you can even take a loss to reduce other taxable income. It is in most people's taxable favor to operate as a business.

Now that you know you are most likely a business and not a hobby in the eyes of the IRS, there is one more thing to consider. According to the IRS, it " . . . presumes that an activity is carried on for profit if it makes a profit during at least three of the last five tax years, including the current year." This means that you can't just start a business in hopes of lowering all your taxable income with lots of losses. By all means, if you have a loss in the start-up years, take those losses, because they are legitimate. Just realize, however, that eventually your business will need to show a profit, or the IRS might come back and say all those losses were just a hobby, in which case you may not deduct those losses from your taxable income.

Most Etsy sellers should lose money only one year or, at most, two years. Etsy is an easy way to have a quick, break-even period of covering your costs with revenues. Many Etsy sellers start making a profit almost immediately. If your business incurs a loss in three out of the past five years, the IRS might treat your business as a hobby and not allow you to deduct your losses. Those who happen to have hobbies that make a profit would report their income on Form 1040, increasing their taxable income.

Okay, now that you know you are a business and have taxable responsibilities, what is the first thing to do?

Federal ID: EIN

I believe one of the best ways to start taking on the tax law is by letting the IRS know you exist and ensuring an identifier is assigned to your business. An Employer Identification Number (EIN) is a type of Taxpayer Identification Number (TIN). You don't have to have employees to get an EIN. I encourage all Etsy sellers to get an EIN, so they don't have to use their Social Security Number

(SSN) when identifying their business. This number is useful for applying for a business checking account and for filling out various state and local small business paperwork that you may typically encounter.

You can be a sole proprietor and use only your SSN and never have to get an EIN. Getting an EIN does not hurt anything or cause you to have to file different taxes or trigger any audit issues—it is simply an ID number. You can apply for an EIN with the IRS online: www.irs.gov/businesses/small/article/0,,id=102 767,00.html.

For more information, I encourage you to read "U.S. Tax Basics: Employer Identification Number," an article I wrote for *Etsy's Seller Handbook*. The article walks you through the benefits and steps of applying for an EIN. Visit www.etsy.com/blog/en/2012/u-s-tax-basics-employer-identification-number/ to read the article in its entirety.

Form 1040

All individuals in the United States file a Form 1040 with the IRS. Form 1040 is the individual-level tax return form and is a good starting point to discover what tax-related responsibilities Etsy sellers face. Taxes are due each year on April 15. Form 1040 is two pages long, but has many individual lines on it. Each one of these lines is a tax topic unto itself. We will focus on four lines (which contain three topics):

- Schedule C (line 12): Business income or (loss)
- Self-employment tax (lines 27 and 56)
- Estimated tax payments (line 63)

Schedule C

Schedule C is the core tax form where sole-proprietor Etsy sellers will spend their time. There is also a shorter form, Schedule C-EZ, but I believe it is best to ignore this form; an Etsy seller might qualify to use it in some years only, whereas in other years he or she would need the full-form Schedule C. Also, you can always use the full Schedule C, but you can get into some trouble if you use the C-EZ when you should have really used the full-form Schedule C. Bottom line: Stick with using Schedule C.

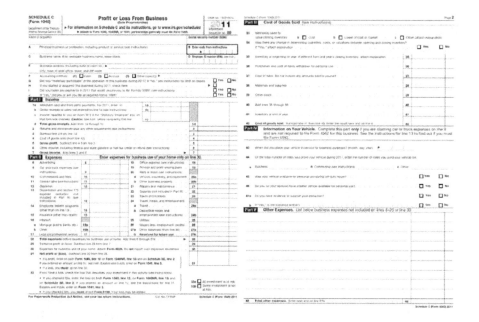

Schedule C is made up of five major sections:

1. Income. This is simply your business's revenue, or all the money you receive during a year. This would include the money your customers pay you for shipping, too.

2. Expenses. This section is where you will record, in many different categories, all the money you spend for your business. This is also where good bookkeeping will really help you with filing your taxes. It is to your benefit to not miss a single expense related to your business, because this will lower your taxable income and save you money.

3. Cost of Goods Sold. This is where you capture how much it costs to make the products that you sold during the year. It includes beginning and ending inventory balances. For example, you sell five dresses for $100 each. Each dress costs you $25 to make, or $125 total (5 × $25). Before the dresses are sold, the $125 is a *cost of goods* (COG). After the dresses are sold, they become *cost of goods sold* (COGS). In this case, the raw material costs of the dresses ($125) are not an expense until they are sold. Once they are sold, they are a $125 expense.

The summary formula for the COGS section on Schedule C is Beginning Inventory Value + New Inventory (purchases, materials, supplies, external labor costs directly related to finished products) – Ending Inventory = COGS. To complete this section, an Etsy seller must take beginning and ending inventory levels (which is really just the inventory level at midnight on January 31). This includes finished and raw materials.

There is an exception to the tax law that allows Etsy sellers to avoid having to complete the COGS section if you have sales under $1 million. This is good news, but it might seem contradictory to what I shared with you in Chapter 3 (where I stated it was beneficial to keep up with inventory levels throughout the year). So, what do I recommend?

I suggest all Etsy sellers keep their bookkeeping by tracking raw material levels, finished inventory levels, and COGS. This helps with pricing and gives an accurate picture of how much profit you are making on a product. It also gives you insight into your inventory levels. But for tax purposes, I suggest you do not follow the COGS method. I suggest that you expense all raw material purchases in the year you purchased them (not in the year the raw materials were sold). This is *cash basis accounting* for tax purposes. This gives your business more expenses and lowers your business's profit, which gives you less taxable income; therefore, you pay fewer taxes. This follows the tax law, lets you pay the least amount in taxes, and gives you great insight with your bookkeeping.

If you desire to use the COGS method for tax purposes to completely match your bookkeeping, this is acceptable. The only difference is that some of your raw material expenses will be captured later, as opposed to immediately. Through the life of your business, these methods will yield similar results (the only difference is a timing difference).

4. **Information on Your Vehicle**. The IRS allows you to deduct certain expenses relating to having a vehicle that helps you conduct your business. The most popular component to track here for Etsy sellers is mileage. Mileage expenses for Etsy sellers (driving to and from craft stores and craft fairs, trips to the post office and to ship products, etc.) are deductible at a set rate for each mile traveled. Specific documentation must be kept to be able to claim this deduction. The rate per mile changes almost every year, so make sure to confirm (at irs.gov) that you are using the correct amount.

5. **Other Expenses**. This section is an open area to capture other types of expenses that don't fit easily into the specific categories in the Expense section.

Ordinary and Necessary

The topic of "ordinary and necessary" expenses is an important concept to understand to make sure you record only proper business expenses. To qualify, a business expense needs to be both ordinary and necessary. *Ordinary expenses* are those commonly accepted for your type of business. *Necessary expenses* are those that are helpful and appropriate for your business. For example, purchasing a desk light for a scrapbook business is ordinary and necessary. Conversely, a trip to the Bahamas for seven days of relaxation and vacation time is *not* ordinary and necessary. The concept is simple. If an expense has nothing to do with your business, don't try to treat it as a business expense. The IRS will catch you on this, and you aren't tricking anyone. The trip to the Bahamas is a personal expense and ignored for tax purposes. Not all purchases for your business are common expenses; they can also be COGS expenses or capital expenses (covered later in the chapter under "Equipment Taxation").

What if you have an expense that is both personal and business-related? For example, say you have an Internet connection that costs $100 per month, and you use it 75 percent of the time for business purposes and 25 percent of the time for personal use. You may deduct 75 percent, or $75, as a business expense. The IRS requires these types of allocations to be documented, so I suggest using a log to track your time. Also, if you are unsure whether an expense is really business or personal, you can always choose just not to deduct it (i.e., do not count it as an expense). This will make your taxable income higher, but you will always be safe in this situation.

Common Etsy Expenses

Here are some expenses that many Etsy sellers might experience in a year of selling. Use these to jump-start your brain to think of all potential expenses. Possible expenses include, but are not limited to, bank fees, advertising, design costs, business cards, signs, flyers, craft show fees, pay-per-click advertising, listing fees on Etsy, PayPal fees, automobile expenses (mileage) consignment fees, copyright fees, other online selling fees, credit card fees, website fees, domain fees, shipping materials, software, travel and entertainment expenses that meet the IRS requirements, business books (including this book), consulting fees, seminars and conferences, accounting fees, tax filing fees, business license fees, office supplies, stationery, equipment, furniture, home-office-related expenses (see under "Home Office Deduction" later in this chapter), membership fees, registration fees, technology purchases, Internet fees, repairs, health insurance, rent, phone, utilities, education, gifts (following IRS rules), professional publications, professional associations, conventions, business travel, parking fees, postage, insurance, contract labor, various services, marketing, social media costs, sales promotions, Etsy search ads, research, security, training, printing, commissions, computer accessories, organization tools, and maintenance fees.

Self-Employment Tax

Self-employment taxes (SE tax) pay for Social Security and Medicare. In a nine-to-five job, these amounts are taken out of your paycheck, and your employer pays part of these on your behalf. When you are self-employed, you have to pay the SE tax on your own. Consider this expense the cost of being your own boss. The SE tax rate is around 15.3 percent (12.4 percent Social Security and 2.9 percent Medicare). These rates can change by year depending on the laws that are passed. There is a threshold at which you will have to start paying the SE tax. If you make more than $400 in profit during a year from your business, you have to pay the SE tax; however, if you have profits below this threshold, you will not have to pay this particular tax. Note: You will have to still file Schedule C for your profits that are below $400. It is important to realize that self-employment taxes are not a deductible expense on Schedule C.

This is the tax that catches many first-time Etsy sellers by surprise. This is a significant percentage of your profits, and the IRS expects you to pay this. In fact, the IRS doesn't want you to pay it only once, at the end of the year; you are expected to pay it throughout the year.

Quarterly Estimated Tax Payments

The IRS has a tax system that is a pay-as-you-go method. This means that as you make profits, the IRS wants you to pay your taxes on this profit four times throughout the year instead of just once. In a nine-to-five job, your employer submits tax payments every three months to the IRS on your behalf. The employer withholds part of your paycheck and sends it to the IRS. As a self-employed individual, it is now your responsibility to do this for your business profits.

There are two ways you can pay your quarterly estimated taxes. First, if you are self-employed only, you will need to file Form 1040-ES four times a year. If you are self-employed and also have a job in which your employer withholds taxes for you, you can have more money withheld by your employer to cover the taxes owed for your small business; if you choose to do this, modify your W-4 with your employer's human resources department or payroll group.

Form 1040-ES	2011 Estimated Tax	Payment Voucher 4	
Department of the Treasury Internal Revenue Service			OMB No. 1545-0074

File only if you are making a payment of estimated tax by check or money order. Mail this voucher with your check or money order payable to "**United States Treasury**." Write your social security number and "2011 Form 1040-ES" on your check or money order. Do not send cash. Enclose, but do not staple or attach, your payment with this voucher.

Calendar year—Due Jan. 17, 2012
Amount of estimated tax you are paying by check or money order.

	Dollars	Cents

Print or type	Your first name and initial	Your last name	Your social security number
	If joint payment, complete for spouse		
	Spouse's first name and initial	Spouse's last name	Spouse's social security number
	Address (number, street, and apt. no.)		
	City, state, and ZIP code. (If a foreign address, enter city, province or state, postal code, and country.)		

For Privacy Act and Paperwork Reduction Act Notice, see instructions on page 8.
Form 1040-ES (2011)   -9-

Estimated tax payments are due on April 15, June 15, September 15, and January 15 for the three months preceding each respective date; for example, taxes for September 1 through December 31 are due on January 15. You can use Form 1040-ES and use your SSN or EIN for identification, or you may pay online. The Electronic Federal Tax Payment System (EFTPS) allows you to pay your estimated taxes, weekly, biweekly, monthly, or quarterly. This allows you to smooth out your payments instead of having one lump sum every three months. The IRS also allows you to make these payments by telephone.

On Form 1040-ES, the IRS provides a sample calculation to help you determine the amount of taxes you might owe quarterly. This exercise will be hardest to perform the first year of running your business. Once you have one year under your belt, you can use the previous year's taxes as a baseline for your current payments. Remember, you are paying all your taxes owed (including self-employment tax).

Sales Tax

There is no one-size-fits-all sales tax rule. Instead, every state has different rules; even local governments have unique rules. This variety of sales tax laws requires me to speak very generically, but I will offer you some knowledge and methods to help you research the sales tax laws that apply to your business. This variety in laws also makes it harder for Etsy sellers to connect and help each other interpret the laws.

Sales taxes are state and local taxes (not federal taxes submitted to the IRS). These taxes are typically a percentage of the sales amount (e.g., 7 percent of a $100 sale is $7 sales tax). Generally, sales tax applies to sales made to customers who are in the same state or local jurisdiction as you. Collecting and filing sales taxes are your responsibility (just like filing your federal taxes), and you might be subject to a sales tax audit to make sure you are filing the proper amount of sales taxes owed. Most states or local taxing authorities require you to have a business ID or business license number created solely for paying your sales taxes that you collect from your buyers. PayPal and Etsy both provide some tools to help you with the collection of your sales taxes. Some groups allow you to collect sales tax in the final price of the item, while others require it to be collected on top of the final sales price. Some taxing authorities might tax inventory levels or equipment. There also might be licenses and permit fees relating to running a business in your state or local taxing authority.

Now that you know a little about the sales tax laws in general, here are some sources to help you research and determine the sales tax laws that apply to your business:

- Find your state's department of revenue website.
- Talk to other local small business owners.
- Call the hotline for your local taxing authority to ask follow-up questions.
- Search the Etsy forums for advice specific to your state (beware of false

information, but it is a good start to find some nuggets of truth).

- Check blogs or websites about your state/local taxing authority.

Here are the questions you should be asking the preceding sources:

- Is there a sales tax that applies to my jurisdiction (state, city, or county)?
- What is the taxing authority for this jurisdiction?
- How often do I have to pay these taxes?
- By what method do I have to pay?
- Is there a small business owner's guide to sales tax for your state's sales tax laws?

Here are some tips to help you deal with sales tax laws:

- Save copies of everything you file (forms might not be as standardized as IRS forms).
- Watch out for fake local or state taxing websites. Since these groups are not as recognizable as the IRS, they are more often impersonated by fraudulent people.
- If you can't research and find all the answers for your specific taxable

situation, seek out a local accountant who can guide you in the right direction.

- I've included a list of state websites on Etsy-preneurship.com for your convenience.

Home Office Deduction

A common, but often overlooked, business tax deduction or expense is the home office deduction. The home office deduction allows you to deduct some expenses relating to your home office. Tax Form 8829 is where you can claim this deduction, but you must follow certain requirements:

- The office must be your principal place of business.
- It must be used exclusively for business purposes (no personal use).
- It must be used on a regular basis.

The room can be a whole separate room or part of a room, but it needs to be a clearly defined place. If you want to create a clearly defined place, you can use dividers in the room or mark it off with some boundary. You must file separate forms if you have a summer home and a winter home. The location that you store your inventory is a little more lenient. You can use a personal space such as a closet shared with personal clothes, but make sure it is separately identified. This deduction can be taken both by those who rent and by those own their home. There are three parts to understanding Form 8829:

1. **Square Footage**. The goal in this section is to determine what percentage of your house or apartment is used for business purposes. For example, you have a home that is 1,000 square feet and use 100 square feet of it for business purposes. Your deduction would be 100 divided by 1,000, or 0.10, which equals 10 percent. This means that you can expense 10 percent as your allowable deduction.

2. **Allowable Deduction**. Some of these deductions include mortgage insurance, real estate taxes, insurance, utilities, repairs, security expense, and maintenance. Renters can count their rent, renter's insurance, and utilities. For example, if you pay $400 a year for a home security system, you would take the $400 and multiply it by the 10 percent, which would equal a $40 home office expense.

3. **Depreciation**. This form also allows you to count the depreciation of your home (not the land) if you desire. Doing this might eventually create taxable gains when you sell your home, so speak with your tax advisor before you include this as part of your home office deduction. (You can just skip this section if you desire.)

Form **8829** — Expenses for Business Use of Your Home
▶ File only with Schedule C (Form 1040). Use a separate Form 8829 for each home you used for business during the year.
▶ See separate instructions.
OMB No. 1545-0074
2011
Attachment Sequence No. 176
Department of the Treasury
Internal Revenue Service (99)
Name(s) of proprietor(s)
Your social security number

Part I   Part of Your Home Used for Business
1 Area used regularly and exclusively for business, regularly for daycare, or for storage of inventory or product samples (see instructions) ... 1
2 Total area of home ... 2
3 Divide line 1 by line 2. Enter the result as a percentage ... 3 %
For daycare facilities not used exclusively for business, go to line 4. All others go to line 7.
4 Multiply days used for daycare during year by hours used per day ... 4 hr
5 Total hours available for use during the year (365 days x 24 hours) (see instructions) ... 5 8,760 hr
6 Divide line 4 by line 5. Enter the result as a decimal amount ... 6
7 Business percentage. For daycare facilities not used exclusively for business, multiply line 6 by line 3 (enter the result as a percentage). All others, enter the amount from line 3 ▶ 7 %

Part II   Figure Your Allowable Deduction
8 Enter the amount from Schedule C, line 29, plus any gain derived from the business use of your home and shown on Schedule D or Form 4797, minus any loss from the trade or business not derived from the business use of your home and shown on Schedule D or Form 4797. See instructions ... 8
See instructions for columns (a) and (b) before completing lines 9–21. | (a) Direct expenses | (b) Indirect expenses
9 Casualty losses (see instructions) ... 9
10 Deductible mortgage interest (see instructions) ... 10
11 Real estate taxes (see instructions) ... 11
12 Add lines 9, 10, and 11 ... 12
13 Multiply line 12, column (b) by line 7 ... 13
14 Add line 12, column (a) and line 13 ... 14
15 Subtract line 14 from line 8. If zero or less, enter -0- ... 15
16 Excess mortgage interest (see instructions) ... 16
17 Insurance ... 17
18 Rent ... 18
19 Repairs and maintenance ... 19
20 Utilities ... 20
21 Other expenses (see instructions) ... 21
22 Add lines 16 through 21 ... 22
23 Multiply line 22, column (b) by line 7 ... 23
24 Carryover of operating expenses from 2010 Form 8829, line 42 ... 24
25 Add line 22 column (a), line 23, and line 24 ... 25
26 Allowable operating expenses. Enter the smaller of line 15 or line 25 ... 26
27 Limit on excess casualty losses and depreciation. Subtract line 26 from line 15 ... 27
28 Excess casualty losses (see instructions) ... 28
29 Depreciation of your home from line 41 below ... 29
30 Carryover of excess casualty losses and depreciation from 2010 Form 8829, line 43 ... 30
31 Add lines 28 through 30 ... 31
32 Allowable excess casualty losses and depreciation. Enter the smaller of line 27 or line 31 ... 32
33 Add lines 14, 26, and 32 ... 33
34 Casualty loss portion, if any, from lines 14 and 32. Carry amount to Form 4684 (see instructions) ... 34
35 Allowable expenses for business use of your home. Subtract line 34 from line 33. Enter here and on Schedule C, line 30. If your home was used for more than one business, see instructions ▶ 35

Part III   Depreciation of Your Home
36 Enter the smaller of your home's adjusted basis or its fair market value (see instructions) ... 36
37 Value of land included on line 36 ... 37
38 Basis of building. Subtract line 37 from line 36 ... 38
39 Business basis of building. Multiply line 38 by line 7 ... 39
40 Depreciation percentage (see instructions) ... 40 %
41 Depreciation allowable (see instructions). Multiply line 39 by line 40. Enter here and on line 29 above ... 41

Part IV   Carryover of Unallowed Expenses to 2012
42 Operating expenses. Subtract line 26 from line 25. If less than zero, enter -0- ... 42
43 Excess casualty losses and depreciation. Subtract line 32 from line 31. If less than zero, enter -0- ... 43
For Paperwork Reduction Act Notice, see your tax return instructions.   Cat. No. 13232M   Form **8829** (2011)

Equipment Taxation

Most Etsy sellers have specific equipment that they use in their business. Common equipment used by Etsy sellers includes computers, cameras, office furniture, photography equipment, printers, and equipment related to their craft (e.g., sewing machines, welding machines). The IRS does not necessarily view these types of purchases as outright expenses. The IRS says these are assets, providing your business with benefits and value over many years. These asset purchases are typically handled in one of two ways:

1. **Section 179 property**. Section 179 property is named after section 179 of the IRS code. Section 179 assets can be fully expensed in the year they were purchased up to the taxable income you have (including other businesses, jobs, or spouse's incomes). These assets need to be primarily for business purposes (more than 50 percent business use). Also, assets purchased from relatives are not allowed to be treated as Section 179 property. Almost every year, Section 179 value limits change, but the good news is that typically most Etsy sellers fall below these limits. Each year, search to find out what the current Section 179 limits are.

2. **Depreciable assets**. This applies to property that is not a Section 179 asset. This type of equipment is purchased in one year, but the expense is allocated through multiple years. This

allocation is called *depreciation*. Typical years of depreciation include three, five, or seven years. For example, you buy a camera for $1,000 and, for some reason, can't treat it as Section 179 property and depreciate it for five years. Each year you have an expense of $200 ($1,000 divided by five years). Section 946 of the tax code can help you determine what category an asset falls into and how many years it should be depreciated. The time of the year you purchase an asset can also influence the convention you use (half year and midquarter are commonly used). These types of assets use depreciation tables that help you determine how much of an asset you depreciate each year. There are various depreciation methods, but they typically can't be changed once they are chosen.

In general, most Etsy sellers will want to use Section 179 assets whenever possible, because this reduces taxable income the most, making your tax bill smaller. Etsy sellers usually have depreciable assets only if they are not able to take advantage of Section 179, either because their total taxable incomes are too low or they purchased more in assets than that year's Section 179 limits.

If you have assets that you use for both personal and business purposes, make sure you keep a log tracking the percentage of time used for each. The IRS requires this documentation and will help you allocate a $1,000 camera that you purchase and use 75 percent of the time for business; this would equal $750 ($1,000 × 75 percent), as per Section 179 property expense.

If you have equipment that you are converting to business use, you should convert it at its fair market value (what it is worth today), not the value at which you purchased it. If you ever sell an asset that you previously recorded for tax purposes, you will need to consider the tax topic of recapture tax. The tax form that walks you through all the details of these topics is Form 4562.

Other Tax Topics

Here are some other important tax-related topics and tips that are helpful for you to know:

- The IRS has a tax advice hotline you can call (1-800-829-4933) to talk to a live IRS employee. I have found these people very helpful in the past. I suggest you call before tax season is in full swing, so you don't have to wait on hold too long. Also,

I suggest you document the person to whom you are talking, the question you asked, and the answer that person provided. Save this as documentation in case you are ever audited on the question you asked.

- There are various ways to file taxes, including paper and pencil (mailing the forms to the IRS), going to a tax filer company, finding a personal tax preparer, free file through the IRS, online tax preparation, and tax preparation software.

I recommend that Etsy sellers use TurboTax to file. I like TurboTax because it gives you specific guidance on tax topics and asks you questions about your taxable situation while you are filing your taxes online. It gives you enough knowledge to be in control and allows you to answer the questions at your own pace (giving you time to research topics if you need to). It also eliminates mathematical errors and puts an expert at your fingertips. It is reasonably priced and professional. I have used it for many years without any problems. I have suggested it to many Etsy sellers and have heard positive experiences from them, too. The version of TurboTax that you use is dependent on your total taxable situation, but the Home & Business version covers the majority of Etsy sellers' needs. You can also file state taxes with TurboTax. If you file electronically, I suggest you print copies of your tax return and save it electronically. One benefit of TurboTax is that it remembers your prior year's tax return and makes using it year after year really easy. I have included a link to TurboTax on Etsy-preneurship.com, as well as some additional tips to filing using this service.

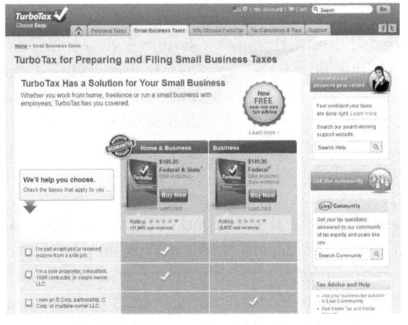

Each year, start filing your taxes early, so you aren't rushed by the April 15 deadline. Answer all questions truthfully, and don't try to pull a fast one on the IRS. Set aside your own personal tax day— it takes time and you don't want interruptions when filing your taxes.

Download: Tax Calculator— Schedule C

Note: To download this document, please go to www.etsy-preneurship.com/downloads.

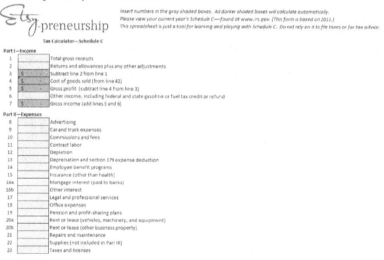

Use this tool to start becoming familiar with the contents of Schedule C. You cannot use this spreadsheet to file taxes, but you can begin by putting estimated numbers in different categories to see how it influences your profit.

Chapter 5

Finances

Managing the finances of your business well leads to financial peace, giving you fewer things to worry about, which allows you to sleep better at night. It can even lead to a competitive advantage over other Etsy businesses. Bookkeeping and taxes have financial elements, but they are mandatory. Governments require you to file taxes. Filing taxes requires you to maintain your bookkeeping. Operating your business with financial excellence is a choice made by the small business owner.

A Tale of Two Financial Approaches

Finances are all the financial affairs that face your business other than taxes and bookkeeping. These can include your bank and PayPal accounts, managing cash flow, how you price your product, financial planning, and other financial pitfalls and tips that separate mediocre businesses from those that thrive. Consider these two hypothetical Etsy sellers' financial stories.

Susan Spendfreely

Susan makes $1,000 in Etsy sales every month; she believes she pays somewhere in the range of $400 in expenses, for a profit of $600. She just spent $2,000 this month buying raw materials to start preparing for the holiday rush in November and December. Susan is well prepared for this surge in sales, but it is only April. Her personal checking account has $2,500 in it. She is not worried about paying for her raw materials at the end of the month. Susan is extremely happy with the quantity of sales she makes each month. In a typical month, she sells 100 products for $10 each. Customer demand is high, and she is selling a lot more products than any other Etsy shop selling related products. Susan feels in control and happy at her business's success.

Three months pass. Susan doesn't have enough money in her personal checking account to pay her monthly rent for her apartment. The number of products she sells each month has increased to 200, but the more sales she makes the less money she seems to have to pay her bills. She has a few more months until the holiday rush, and all her Christmas-themed products are sitting in the corner of her apartment, unable to be converted to cash, because no one is buying Christmas products in July! Susan is worried about her business. She depends on this business for her livelihood—specifically, to pay her monthly grocery bill. She lies awake at night asking herself, "Why are my finances so stressful? My business seems to be doing well, but why can't I pay my bills? I'm so confused."

Megan Moneywise

Megan also makes $1,000 in sales every month and has exactly $400 in expenses, for a profit of $600. She just spent $200 this month buying raw materials to start preparing for the holiday rush in November and December. Megan also plans to spend $600 each month on similar raw materials over the next three consecutive months. Her business checking account has $2,500 in it, and she will easily be able to pay off her business bills, just like she does every month. In a typical month, she sells 25 products for $40 each. Megan doesn't sell as many products as Susan, but is happy with the financial results of her business. Megan is able to transfer $300 every month from her business checking account to her personal checking account. She uses this money to pay for her monthly groceries.

Megan is sleeping well at night. She is able to pay her bills on time. She clearly knows how much cash on hand her business has and how much personal spending money she has. She knows that she can't buy all the raw materials she wants in preparation of the holiday rush all at one time; her budget showed her that she would not have enough cash to do that, so she spaced out the purchases over several months. Her business's finances are thriving. She is managing her finances and feels in control. This peace allows Megan to expand into a new market on Etsy, and this new business idea is booming! Megan feels she might be able to start increasing the money she donates to her favorite charity with her newfound financial success. Maybe she will even purchase that beautiful purse she saw on Etsy last week to reward herself.

Comparing Susan and Megan

There is a clear distinction between Susan and Megan. They both have great operations and marketing strategies, but they manage their finances differently. Unfortunately, Susan's sad story can be quite typical among unprepared Etsy sellers. What is the difference between Susan and Megan? Megan has separate accounts for her personal and business financial accounts and clearly knows where her personal and business cash levels stand. Also, Megan has a financial plan and knows the ups and downs concerning her business's finances, and she is better prepared to know the correct time to make large purchases. Megan also has a pricing formula that tells her $40 is the appropriate sales price to ensure that she is making adequate profit on each sale. Susan is pricing on whim ($10) and is actually losing money on each sale, because she has not considered all the overhead costs of selling her product.

These three separate financial decisions will make Megan a long-term success on Etsy, whereas Susan will quit her business after running it only one year. The lack of separating personal and business funds, lack of budgeting, and pricing issues have soured Susan's hopes and dreams of one day quitting her day job and running her full-time business; it has become a personal financial nightmare that will take her two years to repair. Megan, conversely, has peace and confidence and continues to thrive.

I hear from the Susans almost every day and from the Megans every week. The moment I open up their Etsy convo, I can tell by the tone and the type of questions they ask whether they are starting to lose sleep or are in control of their finances. I love hearing from both the Susans and the Megans on Etsy, because their successes and failures are also my successes and failures. I help the Susans get on the right track financially, so they can turn their finances from disaster to success. I share the joy of the Megans in their implementation of financial practices that I recommended to them earlier, and I enjoy helping them with future financial decisions that face their businesses.

What are the key areas for managing your business's finances well? Good financial management begins with your bank accounts, PayPal accounts, cash management practices, pricing methods, budgeting practices, and other financial pitfalls and tips.

Bank Accounts

Without a doubt, I believe that all Etsy sellers should separate their personal and business bank accounts immediately. This is the smartest and simplest thing you can do to get your finances in order. Benefits of separate checking accounts include:

- *Transparency in ending cash balances.* With separate checking accounts for business and personal funds, you can easily see your levels of cash at any point of time as well as at the end of each month. You will be able to see trends (increasing cash, decreasing cash, or stable cash). These trends will be an indicator to your success. You don't run a business to see decreasing cash or stable cash. A business must make a profit. Businesses that do not make a profit are not sustainable. In the worst case, they lose money or just take up your time with no benefits.

- *Ease of bookkeeping activities.* Monthly bookkeeping transactions are easy to keep track of if they all occur in one place (your business checking account). Having a bank account for only business transactions and a separate bank account for only personal transactions means that you have to look at only your business account to find the transactions you must record. This way, you don't have to sort out personal transactions from your business transactions.

- *Clarity into funding your business.* With separate accounts, you can clearly see the amount of start-up funds you have put into your business. Without a separate account, you can easily lose track. Too many Etsy businesses fail before they have a fighting chance, because start-up costs were not planned, tracked, and adhered to. Spending too much money too early on puts some Etsy sellers in financial holes they have a hard time getting out of.
- *Clarity in transferring profits to personal accounts.* Do not purchase personal items from your business funds. Transfer your profits from your business to your personal checking account and then spend them. Separating these is not only smart for bookkeeping and tax purposes, but also allows you to really see the personal financial gain that your business is providing to you. If you are unable to transfer money out of your business checking account, and you started the business to help pay for personal living expenses, you can see that you are not

meeting your goal. You will then know that you need to make adjustments to the way you run your business.

- *Ease in managing cash flow.* Cash balances move up and down in cycles. Sometimes they go up, sometimes they go down. Awareness of these cycles can help you ration your purchases during peak months to be better prepared for the lean months.

- *Certainty in evaluating financial health.* Cash is a liquid asset, which means it can be easily spent on anything immediately. Raw materials and finished inventories are assets, but are harder to convert to cash—they take time to sell. The ratio of cash to inventory in your business tells you something about your business's financial health. If you build up inventory levels that are too high and barely have any liquid cash, your marketing and operations begin to suffer. The lack of cash limits your ability to take advantage of any business opportunities that arise. At worst, a lack of cash will completely stop your operations and ability to be a business.

- *Confidence during a tax audit.* While a separate business-only checking account is not required by the IRS, it makes any tax audit go smoother when the IRS agent does not see any personal expenses mingled with business expenses. The IRS is concerned that you are deducting personal expenses as business expenses, thus reducing your taxable income. Separate accounts show that these types of transactions are most likely not taking place.

I suggest you open a new business checking account with the same bank that you use for your personal checking account. You can do this online or at a branch of your bank. Although doing this online is easiest, there are some benefits to talking to a small business banker. Knowing this banker gives you a friend at the bank in case your business grows and you have bigger financial needs; bankers know a lot of people and can make excellent networking contacts. Plus, knowing your banker gives you a personal touch with your financial institution of choice.

Most Etsy sellers just need the simplest type of checking account and can ignore many of the costlier, upgraded accounts. Also, consider opening multiple business checking accounts if you have separate businesses or very distinct revenue or expenses that you want to keep separated. I personally use multiple business-related accounts to keep finances separated, which allows for greater transparency in their respective cash flows.

Reconciling bank accounts is another financial operational task to consider implementing. Reconciling is making sure your bank account and bookkeeping are telling the same story. Can you trace all your bookkeeping transactions back to your checking account? Can you trace all your business checking account transactions back to your bookkeeping? If anyone else has access to your funds, reconciling is a simple task that can help you gain trust in that individual; it will help you discern whether that person is spending only what he or she should. Some Etsy sellers find the reconciliation process to be of great benefit in peace of mind, while others see only marginal benefits. I typically reconcile accounts a few times a year to make sure everything is in order and that there are no surprises. The more often I do this, the more confidence I gain in my business's finances.

Paypal

Most Etsy sellers use PayPal as their primary way to pay and receive funds online. I believe all Etsy sellers should also separate their personal PayPal account from their business PayPal account. The benefits of doing this are the same as those accrued by separating personal and business checking accounts: The two are not meant to mingle. Keeping them separate will help ensure the two accounts do not mix. And this will help your financial life immensely.

PayPal has some useful features that Etsy sellers can take advantage of, including:

- *Downloadable CSV spreadsheets of financial activities.* Every month, I log onto my PayPal account and download the monthly activity in a CSV file and save it in my bookkeeping folder. I do this so I have documentation of any transaction that took place that month for tax purposes. The moment I download the data, I have complete control over that data and don't have to trust PayPal to store that data forever. I also see how many transactions took place that month and track this information to view trends. I can easily see how much revenue was received during the month. I can also see how much in fees PayPal took from my sales for offering this online payment service for my business. Use these files to help with your monthly bookkeeping.

- *Shipping labels.* PayPal can help print shipping labels. Be careful that you have up-to-date addresses from your customers. Some people forget to update their PayPal address, and you want to avoid shipping your product to their old address.
- *Sending invoices.* If a customer makes a purchase from your Etsy shop but does not pay you, you can send invoices online to these individuals to remind them to make payment to you. You can also send these types of invoices to any other business owners or customers that you deal with outside of Etsy.
- *Paying bills online.* Many vendors, including Etsy, allow you to pay bills

using your PayPal funds. I personally pay all my bills using a credit card in order to receive the reward points. I then pay off my credit card bill monthly. We'll cover credit cards and bill payment in more detail later in this chapter, but be aware that paying bills directly from PayPal is an option.

- *Monthly transfers to personal or business checking.* Every month, I transfer money from any business PayPal accounts to personal or business checking. Doing this consistently allows you to follow your standards on how much money should be reinvested in your business or taken out as profits ready for personal expenditures or savings.
- *Business/personal identity separation.* When customers make a payment to your PayPal account, they can see some information about you (your name, address, e-mail, and possibly even your phone number). Depending on your comfort level with others knowing such personal information, this can be a possible concern for your identity

protection. There are also various reasons that PayPal could possibly suspend your account, which would lock up your funds. I would much rather have business funds suspended than personal funds suspended. This is another reason to transfer your money to your checking accounts and not build up too large of a balance.

- Sales Tax. PayPal allows for some tracking and management of sales taxes through its features.

Will You Accept Only PayPal?

When I log into PayPal, I see the message, "PayPal. The world's most-loved way to pay and get paid." You can agree with this statement or not, but for many people, this is true. PayPal is the dominant payment method on Etsy. In fact, many Etsy sellers accept *only* PayPal for payment! These Etsy sellers accept payment only through PayPal because it is so convenient. Actually, I am one of these PayPal-only sellers. I have found that most of my customers have a PayPal account and are comfortable paying in this manner. PayPal offers a way for all individuals to pay with their PayPal funds, e-checks, and credit cards. I enjoy my revenues coming into one source (my PayPal account). Therefore, I allow my customers only one method of making payment to me for my products. Has this cost me some sales? It probably has. Has this made my life easier? Yes. Is it the right decision for you? You will have to decide for yourself.

Etsy Direct Checkout

In February 2012, Etsy announced it would begin testing the use of a direct payment checkout system for some Etsy sellers. This would now allow for Etsy customers to directly pay with Visa, MasterCard, American Express, or Discover without going through PayPal. There are both benefits and disadvantages to using this payment method versus PayPal only. These benefits and disadvantages relate to fee structure, average sales price per item, cash flow timing, and shipping considerations. Some Etsy sellers can really benefit from this payment method, while other Etsy sellers might find it more advantageous to stick with PayPal. This decision process is not within the scope of this book, but you should make a well-informed choice. A good place to start would be searching for "direct checkout" in the Etsy News blog.

Types of PayPal Accounts

There are personal, premier, business, and student accounts. I suggest you have a personal account and a business account. You might not need all the services that are offered with the business account right away, but as your business grows, you will probably start using some of these features. Eventually, you can even use advanced merchant capabilities, accepting credit cards directly on your own website or by phone. Businesses can grow faster than you anticipate, so leave room for growth in your PayPal account.

Where Do Those Fees Go, Anyway?

As a consumer, you pay with a credit card and see only one side of the transaction. For example, you go to your local bakery and pay $10 for some breakfast muffins. All you see is a $10 charge on your credit card. The bakery receives the $10, but also has to pay about 30¢ to 60¢ to receive the funds. The bakery really netted only $9.70 or $9.40 for the sale of its muffins. These pennies on the transaction are the cost of accepting credit cards and debit cards for the small business owner. The fees are expenses recorded in their bookkeeping system. What are these fees for, and where do they go?

These fees are called *interchanges fees*. The card companies (Visa, MasterCard, American Express, and Discover) receive some of these fees. The issuers of the cards (think banks or retailers of branded cards) also receive some of these fees. The merchant banker of the bakery also receives some of these fees. In this case, PayPal serves as the merchant banker for most Etsy sellers. PayPal simplifies these fees so it looks like one fee, but there are really many moving parts and fees within this one fee. Thus, transparency in pricing is very limited and also confusing. There are many tiers of pricing based on card type and risks associated with those cards. There is not much for an Etsy seller to do here but accept the fees PayPal charges. The larger your business grows, the more ability you have to negotiate these fees.

Pricing Your Products

One of the first financial dilemmas that Etsy sellers face is how they should price their products. There is no one right or wrong method to pricing products. There is also not one magical formula that works for all sellers. In fact, different types of products probably need different types of formulas. Some products take a lot of time to make; this should be factored into the price of the product/item. Other products have very high material costs that could drive the price higher. Some products are so one-of-a-kind that they can command a premium. Your pricing philosophy that you defined in your business plan (Chapter 2) will also influence your end price. I've seen hundreds of unique pricing formulas used by Etsy sellers. Some are more mathematically based, while others are influenced by market condition and brand. Pricing is both an art and science. I believe both elements are needed to set proper pricing for your business.

The Art of Pricing

The art of pricing is not mathematical. It is based on what similar or related products might be selling for. It is influenced by the brand of your business. This is where pricing can speak quality or value. Some individuals enjoy consistent pricing for all items in their Etsy shop. Different segments of your business's market are willing to pay different prices for the same product. Finding the right price sometimes requires a bit of gut feeling for the market. The magic happens when you find the right price and the right demand (sales). This is where sales can take off and profits increase. A good price is the price that feels fair for both the seller and the customer. Pricing should not be about taking advantage of someone else. Pricing should feel like a win-win situation. Customers are happy with the product at the price they paid, and sellers are happy with the price they received for the product. The art of pricing includes the art of rounding, the psychology of price, and the perception of fairness. The art of pricing is working when the end price feels right. If you focus only on the art of pricing, there is a good chance your prices will not be proper; in fact, doing so may cause you to feel like Susan Spendfreely from the beginning of this chapter. Improper pricing can cause both lack of sales and losing money on each sale you make. Pricing also has an element of science involved. The combination of both the art of science of pricing is what will cause your pricing, and your selling, to be effective.

The Science of Pricing

The science of pricing makes sure that the price pays for the related expenses and provides adequate profit. For an Etsy seller, the cost of a product typically includes the following:

- *Direct raw materials.* If you use $7 of fabric, paint, and beads to make a product, you should be able to directly tie these raw material costs to the creation of your product. This relates to tracking inventory levels and cost of goods when making a product using your bookkeeping system.
- *Common or indirect raw materials.* If you have a jar of glitter you use in a product and use a pinch of it in many products, try to allocate it in some logical manner over the cost of many products. If it is difficult to measure an overall low cost, don't spend hours trying to allocate it just so you can accurately price the product. Other examples might include tissue paper, paint, glue, twine, and thread.
- *Direct costs.* Direct costs are prices you can trace directly to the sale of a product yet are not raw materials. Examples might include boxes for shipping, shipping costs, packing supplies, Etsy listing fees, and PayPal fees.
- *Indirect costs or overhead.* Indirect costs can also be called overhead. Overhead

comprises costs that are not easily traced to one direct product and oftentimes help in the creation of all your products. Examples might include Internet expenses, utilities, gasoline, automobile expenses, equipment, office supplies, advertising expenses, and any other expenses that help you run your business.

Many Etsy sellers include a charge for their hourly labor. This can be a benefit or a disadvantage. Pricing hourly activities can sometimes punish your business's efficiency; some Etsy sellers work faster than others. It is important to note that as a sole proprietor, the IRS does not let you deduct your imaginary hourly wage as an expense for tax purposes. The IRS considers your revenues less your cash expenses to equal your net profit.

Another important aspect to consider when talking about the science of pricing is the wholesale/retail price conundrum that Etsy sellers face when starting to sell off of Etsy. Wholesale price is the price you charge to sell your item to a boutique or store. Retail price is the price you set when you sell an item directly to customers on Etsy or when boutique shops sell it to their customers. Wholesale prices are typically half the retail price, but can range all across the board. Think of the difference between wholesale and retail as a multiplier. When the wholesale price is $10, multiply that by 2, and you get $20 for the retail price. The multipliers can be whatever you or large-volume buyers decide on. Just remember that wholesale prices are negotiable. If wholesalers ask you for a multiplier of 2, request a more favorable multiplier. The worse they can respond is, "No, thanks." If you don't sell anything wholesale, don't even worry about the wholesale price. Instead, just focus on your product's retail price.

Competitor pricing is also part of the science of pricing. If competitors on Etsy sell something similar to your product, and the product quality and all other aspects of your business are similar, you can often become discouraged at their pricing levels. The bottom line is that some Etsy sellers are underpricing themselves out of business as you read this. If they are selling something for $10 that costs you $200 to make, they are either taking a loss, reducing their losses (by selling at a deep discount rather than having it sit in their finished inventory), or have found some really low-cost way to make a product. Use competitor pricing for inspiration, but remember to price in a way that is fair for both you and the customer.

Pricing is not set in stone. If you list an item at a certain price and you have second thoughts about that price level, you can easily change the price. I know many Etsy sellers who are tweaking their prices to find their sweet spot. Most of your customers won't notice that you changed the price of an item. Experiment until you feel comfortable with your prices. You will know you are in the sweet spot of pricing when you stop thinking about it and are making adequate profit and good sales numbers.

The science of pricing also considers your net profit targets. Some sellers might seek to make a lot of profit on selling a few items every month, while others seek small profits on an individual product but hope to make up for it in selling a lot of the products. When Etsy sellers start talking about the science of pricing, the end result is typically a pricing formula.

Popular Etsy Pricing Formulas

Through my time on Etsy, I have encountered hundreds of unique pricing formulas. If you are interested in seeing some of these formulas, I suggest you do some searches through the Etsy forums. These formulas can sometimes be very exact: (price of raw materials × 2.5) + ($6.75 hourly wage × hours worked) + $3 overhead charge + 30 percent of raw material cost for profit markup. (I just made up that pricing formula, so don't feel as though you should use that one.) I am not going to reveal specific Etsy sellers' formulas here, only popular types or concepts of pricing formulas. Then I will reveal what I believe to be a financially sound pricing formula concept that you can adapt to your unique pricing formula.

Cost-Plus Pricing

This pricing method simply takes all costs that can be tracked in some manner (direct and indirect) and adds them together. This number is then multiplied by a percentage markup. Cost-plus pricing = (direct raw materials + indirect raw materials + other direct costs + overhead) × (1 + %). For example, you have a total cost of $100 and a markup of 5 percent. Your price would be ($100) × (1.05) = $105. Benefits of this type of pricing concept are that it is really simple to use. Disadvantages include ignoring the time you spend on the product, psychological pricing mechanics, and effort.

Target Return Pricing

This pricing concept takes you away from looking at one individual product; instead, you would look at selling a lot of one product or would consider everything in your shop as one product. This method requires you to think of net profit as a big-picture item. For example, you want to sell 100 products (they may or may not all be the same, but they are similar). You know the costs are around $500 for all 100 products (or $5 each). You know that when you have sold all of those products, you want a profit of $700. Target return pricing = (cost + target)/(number of products), or ($500 + $700)/100 = $12 per product. This is a $7 markup. Advantages of this method include getting away from pricing individual products that are very similar in cost and having to set a price only once. Disadvantages include possibly selling some of those 100 products at a loss while selling some of your other products are at a higher profit. Some pricing clarity and accuracy may be lost in return for a simpler pricing formula.

Psychological Pricing

Many sellers use a specific pricing formula and then adjust it for the psychological elements. For example, if a woman is determined to buy a particular handbag regardless of its price, she might buy it for $20, $50, or even $250. Price is not that important if someone really wants something. The art of pricing can play into the pricing formula in this element. I know of Etsy sellers who use their pricing formula as a reference point and then finalize the price based on the art of pricing. For example, we calculated the retail price at $12 in the preceding target return pricing formula. If the Etsy seller thinks, "I know $12 is a good price for me, but I have a gut feeling that many customers would love this even at $14." By all means, price it at $14. Your profit will be higher.

The Etsy-preneurship Pricing Formula

This is a pricing formula that I believe is generic enough to be used by all Etsy sellers, yet can easily be customized to be unique to your Etsy shop. The formula works as follows:

Direct raw material costs + indirect raw material costs
   + other direct costs + allocated overhead
   + markup ± psychological pricing adjustments
   = your retail price

The first four parts of the equation are just the definitions of costs we covered earlier (direct raw material costs, indirect raw material costs, other direct costs, and overhead). The operative word here is *allocated*, which means that all overhead costs are spread across many products. This is how I suggest you find your allocated overhead cost:

- *Step 1.* Add up all your overhead costs that can be tied to a month (utilities, Internet, advertising, etc.) and divide these by how many sales you will make during a typical month. For example, you spend $25 a month on utilities for your business, $30 a month on Internet, and $25 on advertising. This is a total of $80 per month. You typically make 40 sales in one month. Divide $80 by 40 products and you get $2 per product on average.
- *Step 2.* Add up any overhead costs that you pay once a year (insurance or annual membership fees). In this case, you spend $200 on insurance and $40 on membership dues, for a total of $240, and $240 divided by 12 months is $20 a

month. Divide $20 a month by 40 sales a month and you get $0.50 per product.

- *Step 3.* Add up any overhead costs that you pay that will last many years. For Etsy sellers, this is typically a computer, a camera, or specialized crafting equipment that will last for three to five years. For example, you buy a computer that costs $500 and a camera that costs $300, for a total of $800. You believe these products will last for five years in your business. During those five years, you expect to sell 2,400 products (5 years × 12 months × 40 = 2,400). Divide 800 by 2,400 products and you get $0.33 per product.

- *Step 4.* Add up your overhead per product calculated in steps 1, 2, and 3 ($2 + $0.50 + $0.33 = $2.88 per product). This is your allocated overhead. This $2.88 allocated overhead cost might end up being ridiculously high if you are selling a low-priced item, but this can be adjusted in the psychological pricing adjustment section of the formula.

Allocating Overhead

Step 1. Monthly overhead	→	
Step 2. Annual overhead	→	Step 4. Overhead per product
Step 3. Long-term overhead	→	

The next key part of this pricing formula is to define markup. You have the freedom to choose how you mark up. You can mark up in a similar method to cost-plus pricing described previously, or you can even mark up based on paying yourself an imaginary hourly wage (rate × hours). Another possibility is setting a fixed markup price, such as the used $7 in the target return pricing example. The markup portion of the formula is customizable by you to meet your specific needs. You can mark up with none, one, some, or all of these methods.

The last part of this pricing formula is an adjustment up or down for pricing psychology. Do whatever you want that is related to the art of pricing here to arrive at your final price, but just make sure you are not selling your items at a loss, unless you have a good reason to do so.

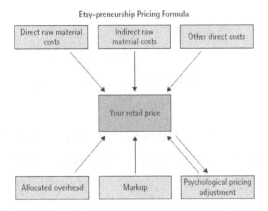

Etsy-preneurship Pricing Formula

Notes on Pricing for Jewelry Products

Etsy sellers who make jewelry often have a difficult time at arriving at a final price for their items. First, the products may contain rare and expensive minerals, gems, or stones. Some of these materials' prices might be fluctuating daily (silver, gold, platinum prices). Second, many of these sellers have some items that are easily traced for direct material costs, while other, low-cost, items are tracked as indirect costs. Some Etsy sellers track each individual bead and its cost, while other sellers track only the expensive beads. I am aware of some Etsy sellers who find the average cost per bead. Other sellers allocate costs based on weight of the product. All of these methods have their benefits and disadvantages. The bottom line is that Etsy sellers must pay a great deal of attention to detail when managing their inventory and pricing for jewelry; they must set clear expectations and pricing formulas that are both appropriate and reasonable.

Getting Feedback on Your Pricing

I suggest all sellers seek some feedback on their pricing formula. Here is how I suggest you get this feedback. First, create and tweak a pricing formula until you feel good about the pricing it generates. Then ask friends, family, and coworkers to look at your product pictures and descriptions. Ask your trusted critics to write down the price they think you asking for that product. Then ask them, "How much would you spend to purchase that item?" You will be surprised at the results from various individuals. Some perceive your products as really expensive, and others think you should give them away free or at a loss.

Finally, show them the product pictures and the prices you created, and get their reaction to those prices. The prices you see in stores and in online shops are often the result of evaluations similar to this process. As consumers, we see prices all the time, and we are good at evaluating them; in fact, we usually immediately know whether the price is good or bad for us, unrealistic, or a bargain. These reactions can help you hone your pricing skills. When it comes to pricing, use both the art and the science, all while trusting your pricing instincts.

Budgeting

Budgeting allows you to see what the future might hold for your business's finances. It is typically based on the assumption of growth and thus forecasts key financial areas at a high level. Key financial areas to budget include sales, expenses, raw material levels, finished inventory levels, and cash. Looking out 12 to 18 months is a good budget. That time period is long enough to help you see what general trends might be happening for your business, but it is not so far out that it is completely unrealistic. Budgets can help you plan where you want your business to be in the future. If your actual results differ from what your budget states, you can adjust part of the way through the budget. A budget can also help motivate you to achieve your challenging business growth. When creating a budget, don't worry about whether your assumptions are incorrect, just make your best educated guess. Planning helps you deal with uncertainties that you may face regarding your business and its future.

Managing Your Cash

Every business must learn how to manage its cash. The key part of managing cash is actually managing the flow of the cash. One of the most quoted reasons that small businesses fail is cash flow problems. This is a broadly stated issue, but in the business world there is a famous phrase: "Cash is king!" An Etsy shop's cash transactions can tell you a lot about a business. Etsy sellers should manage and track four types of cash flows:

1. *Inflows*. Inflows are all the sales revenue your business receives. They flow into your business and increase your business cash balance.

2. *Outflows*. Outflows are all the expenses or costs your business pays out. They flow out of your business and decrease your business cash balance.

3. *Funding flows*. Funding flows occur when you take your personal cash and put it into your business. They flow into your business and increase your business cash balances. (Note: For sole proprietors, the IRS does not consider funding flows as existing, because there is no separation between the business and the owner. As a sole proprietor, you and the business are one.) Almost all Etsy sellers begin their business with a funding flow to start having some money to spend on business activities.

4. Payout flows. Payout flows occur when you take money out of your business cash and transfer it to your personal account. They flow out of your business and decrease your business cash balance. (Note: For sole proprietors, the IRS does not consider payout flows as existing, because there is no separation between the business and the owner. As a sole proprietor, you and the business are one.) Payout flows must eventually happen for all businesses, unless the business owner continues to reinvest all profits back into the business to help the business grow larger. Many Etsy sellers intentionally reinvest their profits for a number of years to help their business grow larger and become more stable in their operations.

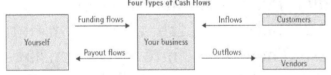

Four Types of Cash Flows

Three Financial Mistakes to Avoid

Here are some of the worst financial mistakes I have seen Etsy sellers make through the years.

These mistakes are not technical errors (tax laws, bookkeeping disciplines, or math miscalculations), but are instead mental games of financial self-control, limits, and planning.

Not Having Financial Boundaries in Place

There are borders around sandboxes and fences around the parks. Why are these boundaries in place? They are there to keep children from playing on a busy street and getting hurt. Financial freedom does not mean spending whatever you want, whenever you want, on whatever you want. Financial freedom means doing whatever you please within prescribed financial boundaries you have set for yourself. Financial boundaries allow you to have better self-control over your finances, because you play within the rules. The rules are in place only to serve and protect you. Financial boundaries can include budgets, monthly spending limits, designations of net profit to reinvest or pay out, financial goals, financial limits, debt ceilings (maximum amounts of debt), and loss limits.

Not Knowing When to Call It Quits

While running a small business, it is important to know when to call it quits. Through the years, I've started and stopped quite a few business ventures. One benefit of being a sole proprietor is that you can move fairly fast to see whether something is going to be a hit or a bust. Unfortunately, not every Etsy business will make it. I do believe that every person can find an Etsy business that thrives, but it might require someone to mess up and learn some things along the way. There are no one-size-fits-all answers that tell you when to call it quits. Here are a few guidelines I use to evaluate whether it is time call it quits on a business venture.

- *You have lost a designated amount of money.* When you start a venture, you can set a financial boundary or a loss limit. A *loss limit* is a set amount of money that you will lose in the attempt to make a profit. For example, you set a loss limit of $2,000. Through the next four months, your business spends $2,000 but does not make a single sale. Your financial boundary states that you will not spend any more money. If you can't see the progress you are looking for with a certain monetary threshold or time limit, you can call it quits.

- *You don't have any other ideas to try.* If you can quit your business and have no regrets, you can feel safe knowing you did everything possible to succeed. If you always made the best decisions at given points in time and have no more ideas to test to make your business succeed, you have done your best.
- *The market has spoken no.* If your customers are not responding and you have tried various branding techniques, price points, and pictures, the market has spoken no. Customers decide which businesses are successes or failures. If customers never respond to your business, it might be time to try something else.
- *Counsels with others have spoken no.* Entrepreneurs tend to be fairly passionate about their businesses. In fact, the business and the individual are oftentimes thought of as the same thing. Find a few people in your life whose advice and wisdom you trust. Ask them

what they think about your business and seek feedback. Sometimes, the best way to get a fresh perspective is to see your business through the eyes of someone else.

There are benefits to failing or succeeding fast with a small business. If it is a failure, learn from it and move on and try again. There is also a time to ignore the drumbeat of "calling it quits" and to persevere and keep trying. Decisions like these are always from the heart, and each individual will know when to keep going even though the future looks difficult.

Not Counting the Costs of Quitting Your Day Job

Many Etsy sellers hope to one day quit their day job and run their own full-time business. This is a noble pursuit, but it is not something to be decided upon lightly. There are occasions for rash decisions, but I believe quitting your day job to run an Etsy business is not one of these occasions. The costs must be counted, and there are things you can do over multiple years to help you prepare for the possibility of that day. Financial planning is the best thing to help you see whether you are ready to quit your day job. Create budgets for personal and business spending and revenue, and observe how your finances would look in various situations.

If you do hope to one day quit your day job and run your own full-time business, here are some steps I believe you should be taking now in preparation for that day. First, consider getting rid of any personal debt you might have before becoming a full-time Etsy seller. Second, look for ways to reduce your personal expenses. Third, create a cash reserve as a safety net. Fourth, diversify where your revenues come from. Fifth, create semipassive income opportunities, if possible.

Financial Tips

Here are a few more financial topics I think are worth briefly covering to make sure you have the best possible financial future for your business.

- *Starting on a financial shoestring.* If you can start up a business using only $500 versus $5,000, see whether you can succeed by putting only $500 at risk. Don't buy unnecessary equipment right away when starting a business. I know it can be tempting to buy all new office furniture, crafting desks, computers, cameras, and supplies with the hope of starting a business. Start the business and save these types of expenses until later, after you have tasted some success.

- *Paying bills.* Create a monthly schedule to pay off your business bills once per month. Pay your bills as part of your bookkeeping cycle. Don't let bills become past due.
- *Using credit cards.* If you can responsibly use a credit card for your personal finances, use one for your business as well. If you can't use a credit card responsibly for your personal finances, you most likely will not be able to use one for your business, either. I use credit cards for almost every purchase, but I use them with discipline. For myself, using credit cards is convenient, groups all my expenses in one place, and helps me earn rewards. I pay off all credit card balances when they become due. It is a tool for managing my expenses, not something that puts me into debt.

- *Using debt in your business.* Set standards about the debt in your business (how much debt, how long you will take to pay it back, how long you will keep it, where you will generate the debt). If you intentionally decide to go into debt, always have a plan to pay it off. Consider saving up the money you need to start your business instead of funding it with debt. Debt has its place, but it can put limits on your business quickly.
- *Spending money to make money.* I have had to warn some Etsy sellers to put limits on their spending, per my first tip, "starting on a financial shoestring." The truth is, however, that not all Etsy sellers love to spend. If you are tight, frugal, or just a tightwad, you might need to open your wallet a little wider while running a business. Creating and running a successful business requires you to spend some money to make money. Don't let your fiscal personality cause your business to be starved of the financial resources it needs.

- *Taking calculated financial risks.* Starting and running a business can be risky. You must look for calculated risks that have low downside but high upside opportunities. Each Etsy seller has different risk tolerance levels. You must understand your risk personality type and operate accordingly. If you are a big risk taker, find a way to limit the number of risks you take and focus on taking only the best possible risks. If you are a small risk taker, look for opportunities to take larger calculated risks.

Download: Pricing Tool and Formula

Note: To download this document, please go to www.etsy-preneurship.com/downloads.

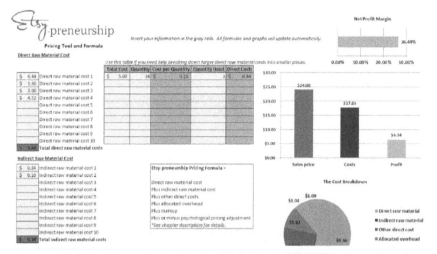

First, use this tool to play around with various pricing formulas you create. Then decide on a pricing formula you will use consistently. You can have different pricing formulas for different types of products. Use this formula when pricing the new products you create.

Chapter 6

Legal

The law provides social order to regulate our conduct and interactions between each other. There are laws that dictate how your business interacts with the government, other businesses, and your customers. Law is constantly evolving in its attempt to better serve individuals and groups of people. In this chapter, the following important legal topics for small business owners are covered:

- How businesses can be structured
- Understanding the basics of contracts
- Understanding intellectual property laws
- Business insurance (managing risk)
- Other legal topics important for Etsy sellers

Choosing Your Business Structure

All businesses must be structured or formed in some manner. Sole proprietorship, partnership, single-member limited liability company (LLC), cooperative, S corporation, and C corporation are all types of business structures. The three types of business structures that are most common on Etsy include sole proprietors, partnerships, and single-member LLCs. Each of these business structures has unique characteristics that differentiate it from the others. Their key differences are related to legal liability and how they are taxed. These differences will help you see the benefits and disadvantages of the different types. The majority of Etsy sellers operate as sole proprietors. Etsy sellers who work with other individuals usually comprise a partnership. Those individuals who desire greater liability protection form an LLC. Ideally, you should choose the type of business structure you'd like to form before starting your business. It is helpful to know some of the specifics of your business structure type; this will give you a better understanding about how the law views your business for taxation and liability purposes.

Sole Proprietor

This business structure easily represents the majority of sellers on Etsy. The business and the person starting the business are one entity, with no separation between them. These are easiest to form, and you are your own boss. Sole proprietorships can be full-time or part-time businesses. Sole proprietorships can be small or large (even having their own employees). Sole proprietors are liable for all business debts and financial obligations of the business. If a customer were to sue your business, he or she is also suing *you*, with no segregation or separation of your business and personal assets. Sole proprietors file Schedule C with the IRS and are subject to paying self-employment taxes. Taxes might need to be paid quarterly through the year.

Partnership

If you and another person or a group of people join together to run a business, you have most likely entered into a partnership. Each of these individuals provides their skills, labor, money, or assets to help the business succeed, and each person then shares the financial rewards or losses. Three types of partnerships include general partnerships, limited partnerships, and joint ventures.

Of the Etsy sellers that are partnerships, I have observed most to be general partnerships. General partnerships assume that everything is shared equally (unless documented in the partnership agreement). Limited partnerships work together, but with some liability protection. A joint venture is a business project that takes place for a limited amount of time to accomplish a purpose. There is no separation of liability between the business and the individuals in a partnership. In fact, as a partner, you are also liable for the actions, debts, and legal liability of the other partners! Choose your partners carefully.

Partnerships file an informational return to the IRS (Form 1065). The income is passed through to each individual very similarly to a sole proprietorship. Partners generally have to pay self-employment taxes as well as quarterly estimated taxes. Partnerships allow you to increase the skills and capacity of your business, but they also increase your liability risk, because you are working with other individuals whom you do not control. Partnerships have a greater chance to fail due to interpersonal conflict.

Limited Liability Company (LLC)

This business structure allows owners to have limited personal liability for all the actions performed and the debts accrued by the LLC. The IRS does not view an LLC as an official classification for tax purposes. The IRS lets the LLC check a box to choose to be treated as a sole proprietor, a partnership, or a corporation for tax purposes. Of the LLCs that I have come across on Etsy, most are sole proprietor types, filing Schedule C. The main benefit of LLCs is the limited liability protection it provides. If someone sues your business, your liability is tied up in the assets and investments of the business. This type of structure does provide some protection, but remember, if you as an individual cosign a loan as an individual, you will still be personally liable. Also, an LLC member can be held personally liable for fraud or misrepresentations, through the act of "piercing the corporate veil." Forming an LLC is somewhat complicated, and you may have some start-up costs and annual fees. You can file paperwork to become an LLC online (links provided on the Chapter 8 web page of Etsy-preneurship.com).

Tips on Choosing a Structure

As a small business owner, you can always start up as a sole proprietor and become an LLC in the future if you desire the greater liability protection. The extra liability protection is an indicator of your risk-tolerance level being low. Most Etsy sellers are never sued, making the sole proprietorship easy and appropriate. However, I believe that the small percentage of Etsy sellers who *are* sued wish they would have opted for the liability protection of an LLC. Every business owner's case is unique, and if you think you need additional commentary and feedback, definitely seek out the wisdom of a legal counselor who can give you advice on your business structure.

Contracts

Contracts are the language of how business gets done. Small business owners encounter all types of contracts, and it is helpful to know a little about contracts and their composition to better understand and negotiate them appropriately. Knowledge is power in negotiations, and knowing the law regarding contracts can help you negotiate the most favorable terms for your business. Contracts are a part of our everyday lives, from the gym membership you sign to the credit card receipt you sign after a meal, and everything in between.

Necessary Elements of a Contract

All contracts must contain three elements—offer, acceptance, and consideration—and all contracts require competency, consent, and legality.

- *Offer.* One person proposes a deal, which is communicated in a clear manner to another person. The offer remains open until it is accepted, rejected, retracted (taken back), or expires, or until a counteroffer closes the original offer. Offers contain terms, or the details of the agreement.
- *Acceptance.* The person who received the offer acknowledges to the person who made the offer that the offer is accepted. Acceptance must be made in the manner dictated in the offer.
- *Consideration.* The bargained-for exchange is that both individuals must give up something and receive something. To identify the consideration you can fill in the blanks: "I give you ____ for ____. You give me ____ for ____."
- *Competency.* This is common sense, but you should make contracts only with

someone who is of sound mind. Also, be sure this person is at least 18 or older.
- *Consent.* Do both parties agree to the terms of the contract? Make sure you understand all the details of a contract before giving consent. Misunderstanding the terms is one of the most disputed elements of contract law. The terms are binding, even if you did not understand them when signing.
- *Legality.* You cannot make a contract to perform an illegal activity.

Commonsense Contract Tips

Here are some contract tips, which I've developed through years of working with many contracts, that I believe are of particular use to Etsy sellers:
- Always put the contract in writing and have it signed by both parties.
- Don't be afraid to use common language in a contract. You don't have to talk like a lawyer to write a good contract.
- Read every word of every contract you sign, and understand the contract in its entirety.

- In most cases, negotiate for better terms. The worst the other party can say is no.
- Let your yes mean yes and your no mean no. Fulfill any contracts you enter.
- Keep a file folder of all your business contracts for future reference.
- Peruse some of the many useful, free, online small business contracts that cover a variety of topics.
- Use contracts as a tool to help you meet your business's needs. Spell out your expectations for the other party in a clear manner.

Intellectual Property

Etsy is a website where thousands of creative individuals sell products. Most of these sellers create some type of intellectual property, which includes patents, trademarks, trade secrets, trade symbols, trade names, and copyrights. The combination of creativity and competition in one place brings out the best and worst in some individuals. Given enough time, almost all Etsy sellers will at some point find someone copying their work, or they will be accused of copying someone else's work. Knowing the basics of intellectual property law will give you a firm foundation when these troubling moments face your business.

Intellectual property laws exist to give business owners the confidence to invest in creating new things. If it were okay to be a copycat, there would be no incentive to be original; it would also discourage business owners from taking any risks, because there would be no protection, and people could imitate your business.

Copyrights

Copyright law is the one area of intellectual property that I suggest you read about the most. Copyrights provide protection to the author of an original work of authorship. This can include written words, dramatic works, music, art, and certain other intellectual works. Works can be published or unpublished and still be protected by a copyright. Copyright laws are national laws. There is no such thing as an international copyright. Spend some time on copyright.gov to learn all about the copyright law in the United States. I suggest every Etsy seller spend at least an hour reading this site to become familiar with what the copyright law protects and does not protect. Develop a plan for protecting your copyrights. Registration of a copyright is not required in order for a work to be protected by the law; the copyright exists the moment the work is fixed in a tangible medium. If you do register a copyright, it gives you additional remedies for copyright infringement. Generally, the copyright must be registered to sue for infringement. Copyright laws protect the original expression of an idea; they do not protect ideas, procedures, processes, systems, methods of operation, discoveries, concepts, or principles. It is advisable to speak to your legal counsel if you have concerns about your business's copyrights.

Trademarks

Trademarks make businesses identifiable from each other. Trademarks can include words, phrases, symbols, designs, or any combination of these. For an authoritative document that you as an Etsy seller should read, visit www.uspto.gov/trademarks/basics/BasicFacts_with_correct_links.pdf for a wealth of information about trademarks and how they may relate to your business.

Patents

Patents are not very common on Etsy, but they protect inventions or processes. It is possible to patent a utility, a design, or a plant. The United States Patent and Trademark Office (uspto.gov) has useful details regarding patents.

Trade Secrets

Many businesses have some operational secrets that are commercially valuable. These could include your customer lists, secret processes, or methods used in the production of goods. Independent research or inspection of a finished product by competitors is not illegal. Most products sold on Etsy can be figured out by others. The moment you post a picture of something, most people already have a good idea how it was made.

Small Business Insurance

All businesses have risks that can impact their operations. These risks can range from being sued over misuse of a product to having your house burn down and losing your entire finished inventory. The majority of Etsy sellers do not have business insurance coverage; however, I am aware of some Etsy sellers who, as their businesses grow larger, do purchase insurance to manage the risks that face their respective businesses. The decision to purchase or skip insurance depends on your level of comfort with risk. Remember, when purchasing insurance, get quotes from multiple insurers to make sure you are getting a competitive price. Also, look for discounted bundles where you might be able save money by purchasing all of your insurance from one provider. One alternative to insurance is to self-insure by keeping a cash reserve for times of uncertainty.

The Etsy shops that do have insurance are typically the Etsy shops that are more successful. These business owners tend to run their Etsy shops as a business and realize that risk management is an important part of ensuring the continuing success of their business. Generally, 40 percent of small business owners have business insurance, but I believe this percentage is much smaller for Etsy sellers. Business insurance is not often discussed in the Etsy community, but it should be considered, or at least be on your radar, for future implementation.

Types of Insurance

Here are various types of insurance coverage that can be useful for Etsy sellers:

- *Business owner's policy (BOP).* This insurance coverage is typically a combination of property insurance and liability insurance
- *Property insurance.* This insurance covers your business's inventory, equipment, and supplies.
- *Business insurance on liability.* This insurance covers legal expenses to defend yourself and protects some of your assets if your product were to harm someone.
- *Business insurance on commercial auto.* If you use a vehicle for your business, you should have auto insurance.
- *Errors and omissions business insurance.* This insurance covers you when customers claim your services caused them harm.
- *Umbrella business insurance.* This insurance is additional coverage beyond your BOP, usually offered at a lower price.

- *Workers' compensation business insurance.* If you have employees who work for you, you should consider having a workers' compensation policy. It provides wage replacement and medical benefits to employees who are injured while they work for you, and the employee also gives up some rights to sue you for negligence.
- *Specialized industry business insurance.* If you perform a dangerous craft (high fire risks or hazardous chemicals), you might seek out special insurance for your craft.
- *Product liability claims.* Your product consists of the product, the shipping materials, the instructions, labels, and advertising. Make sure they all are safe and will not cause your customers' harm.
- *Medical insurance.* If you are not covered by health insurance and are self-employed, you will need to consider purchasing medical insurance.
- *Other.* If you can dream up the risk, there is a good chance that an insurance company can create a policy to cover it.

- *Avoiding risk.* Another way to insure against risk is to purchase something that will help you avoid the risk in the first place. For example, you could purchase virus and malware protection for your computer and keep it updated. This is a wise investment, and I have seen infected computers shut down Etsy businesses for periods of time.

Other Legal Topics to Consider

Here are a few other legal topics that Etsy sellers should be aware of, many of which are occasionally discussed in the Etsy forums.

- *The Consumer Product Safety Improvement Act (CPSIA).* This has been a popular topic for Etsy sellers who create products for children. At a very high level, CPSIA, a law passed in 2008, imposes new testing and documentation requirements and material safety on the manufacturing of several different types of product. There is an Etsy team devoted to this topic. The law is quite controversial, because it places a lot of hardship on small business owners.

- *Gift cards.* Selling gift cards for your Etsy shop is a great way to increase sales, but you must be aware of any local laws that might regulate how you sell and handle gift cards. There are some great articles on Etsy's blog (www.etsy.com/blog/en/2010/how-to-offer-gift-certificates-in-your-etsy-shop/) about how to offer gift cards in your Etsy shop online.
- *Food.* Selling food is a business that has additional regulations. Start with local regulations, move up to state regulations, and then look at any federal regulations. The Food and Drug Administration (FDA) sets the national guidelines. You might need permits; you might need to have a commercial kitchen; you might be required to be inspected by regulators. There are also laws that indicate how you will need to label your foods.
- *Privacy laws.* The moment you make your first sale, you are entrusted with information that is private. You know what customers purchased, their names, their e-mail addresses, how they paid,

and possibly their telephone numbers. Customers purchase from you in trust— this includes sales to famous people (Hollywood loves Etsy)! You should keep this information private, as it would be terrible publicity for your business if it were to become known that you did not respect a customer's privacy. Also, consider making a privacy policy for your website, because it gives confidence to your customers that you respect their privacy and have operational standards that are reputable.

- *Cease and desist (C&D).* A cease-and-desist letter can be written by lawyers or another business owner to tell you, "Stop this business activity or you might face legal action." C&D can also come from judges. Etsy sellers typically run into C&Ds for intellectual property problems. Don't act like you are Coca-Cola if you are not. Don't sell products you make using patterns that are not for resale. Don't sell products that are copyrighted.
- *Business names.* There are many laws, regulations, and requirements that come

with choosing a business name. The Small Business Administration (SBA) has a great article on these requirements (go to www.sba.gov/content/how-name-business).

- *Legal help when you need it.* The moment a legal issue is filed or threatens your business, many people feel frustrated and oftentimes don't think clearly. This is where the benefit of good legal counsel will make a world of difference. Find an attorney or someone else whom you trust, who knows the law, and who will be able to help you think clearly. Prepaidlegal.com comes with recommendations for legal help from other Etsy sellers. You prepay to use the services on Prepaidlegal.com when you need such advice.

- *Ignoring the law.* It does an Etsy seller no good to be aware of the law and just choose to ignore it. For example, I've seen Etsy sellers say in the forums something along the lines of, "I knew the law, but did not think it was that serious. I never thought I would get caught—until I did."

- *Small-claims court.* This is an easier way for Etsy sellers to resolve small disputes at a low cost. You typically represent yourself in small-claims court. There is a good article on the basics of small-claims court featured on Nolo.com, a well-regarded legal website (www.nolo.com/legal-encyclopedia/small-claims-court).
- *Contest law.* Be aware that there are laws that regulate any contests your business might sponsor.
- *Uniform Commercial Code (UCC).* This governs leases, contracts, borrowings, money, and the sale of goods—all things many Etsy sellers come into contact with frequently. The UCC is state law. Check out www.law.cornell.edu/uniform/ucc.html for applicable laws.
- *Advertising law.* There are laws detailing how you may advertise, including truth-in-advertising laws and laws about labels on products.
- *Copyright common sense.* Don't use Mickey Mouse on your products or NFL

team logos, because you do not own them. You will eventually be forced to remove such infringements and your shop may be shut down. Many large companies search Etsy for copyright infringements.

Following Etsy's Rules

Etsy is where your business lives, and just as you may have house rules for your home, Etsy has rules for selling on its venue. Etsy has terms, do's and don'ts, a privacy policy, and states how it will handle any copyright issues. Read these rules (go to www.etsy.com/help/article/483), and make sure you obey them. You must play by Etsy's rules to sell on Etsy. Etsy shops are shut down or suspended for not following the rules.

When you are selling on Etsy, you do give up some control over how your business is run. Your business is on Etsy, and, although I think Etsy will be around for the foreseeable future, you must protect your business from any unknown circumstances that might result in Etsy no longer being your business's selling place. Etsy is a business, and businesses can fail. Make sure you have copies of your banner and avatar. Save all your product description write-ups in documents. Keep copies of all your product pictures. Keep a document with some of your best feedback. Purchase a domain name so you can sell on your own site; and have a plan of action in case something out of your control happens to Etsy or your Etsy shop. A little preparation can go a long way if disaster ever strikes your business.

Small Business Ethics

Ethics is moral philosophy, and there are many different studies of ethics to try to help determine what is right or wrong. As a small business owner, you will develop your own ethical standards of operations. These standards will be different for many individuals, but also have many overlapping areas.

I have actually tried to define many of my ethical standards in writing. I encourage you to try to write out the principles on which you run your business. Your value statement from Chapter 1 would be a good place to start.

Download: Business Structure Quiz—Finding Your Perfect Fit

Note: To download this document, please go to www.etsy-preneurship.com/downloads.

Etsy-preneurship

Select your answer (A, B, or C) for the following 10 questions.

Business Structure Quiz—Finding Your Perfect Fit

1. When it comes to understanding legal issues, filing paperwork, and starting a business:
   A. I want it to be as easy as possible.
   B. I don't mind some paperwork to file with my partners.
   C. I am not intimidated by paperwork and handle bureaucracy well.

2. When it comes to filing taxes, I prefer:
   A. the simplicity of my business profits rolling up to be taxed with my personal taxes.
   B. to share the income with those I work with.
   C. to choose to be taxed as a sole proprietor, partnership, or corporation.

3. When it comes to my business's operations, I plan on:
   A. selling my creative product made by myself.
   B. working with my partner to offer creative products.
   C. turning my creative business into a huge empire.

4. When it comes to funding my business, I hope to:
   A. provide all the funding from my own savings and personal debt.
   B. provide some funding along with contributions from my partners.
   C. provide some funding myself, but also be able to receive money from other investors.

5. When it comes to my personal assets being legally at risk, I prefer:
   A. my personal and business assets being the same thing.
   B. being legally liable for actions my partners take.
   C. having some separation between business and personal assets.

6. When it comes to debt and my business, I prefer:
   A. to consider my business-related debts as personal debts.
   B. to be personally liable for any debts my partner enters into on our behalf.
   C. to have that debt be directly tied to the business.

7. When it comes to working with others in my business, I prefer:
   A. to work alone, hire independent contracts, or have a few employees.
   B. to work with partners.
   C. flexibility in working alone, hiring independent contracts, and having many employees.

8. When it comes to my business, it is important for my customers to think of me as:
   A. an independent artist working for myself.
   B. a group of like-minded people working together.
   C. a formal business that is more structured than a sole proprietorship.

9. When it comes to selling my business, I could see myself:
   A. never wanting to really sell it. I am my business.
   B. selling out my share to my partners.
   C. selling the business formally to someone else.

10. When it comes to forming a business, I prefer:
    A. forming a business in the easiest way possible.
    B. forming a business that has the greatest chance of historic failure, but greater synergy with partners.
    C. taking my time for some benefits, but also having start-up costs and an annual fee.

Scroll down to see your results. No cheating! First, answer all 10 questions.

You can use this quiz as a starting point in deciding which type of legal structure is right for your business. Make sure to take your time and research the benefits and implications of each

business structure type, and seek outside counsel
if needed.

Chapter 7

Operations

Operations are the daily tasks that you perform to make your business function. Operations are the work you perform and the sweat of your brow, and they take up the largest percentage of your time as a small business operator. Operations include making products, photographing products, managing your Etsy shop, communicating with customers, shipping out products, ordering raw materials, providing feedback, writing product descriptions, providing customer service, performing your bookkeeping, keeping your workspace clean, managing your schedule, and hundreds of other tasks that make up an Etsy seller's day.

Operations look different for every seller on Etsy, because everyone has a different way of achieving these tasks. Sellers have different ideas of what is important and value different operational tasks above others. One Etsy seller might consider product photography as a more important task than writing product descriptions. This value might be more prevalent in an Etsy shop with great photos that demand attention, but when you view the product to read the description, you might find misspelled words and incomplete sentences; you might desire a more explanatory verbal product description. Your business operations could very well influence whether your business fails or succeeds, and they will definitely impact both you as a small business owner and your business's customers.

Why Operations Matter

We've already realized that there is no one perfect way to operate your small business, but we can we find clues by looking at how the most successful Etsy businesses owners operate and what techniques help them run great Etsy shops.

Through the years of running my own Etsy business and interacting with thousands of Etsy sellers, I have found what I believe to be the secret of good operations: *consistency*. Consistency makes people feel safe and secure, provides clear expectations, and allows you to maximize your potential. All these benefits impact both you and your customers in important ways.

Personal Impact

Small business owners add hundreds of tasks to their everyday life that would not exist if they did not run a business. More tasks usually equate to more time demands and additional stressors. Offsetting these hardships are the rewards and benefits a small business brings to the owner. In the end, you hope the benefits of operating a small business outweigh its costs. Just as you hope your revenue is greater than your expenses, giving you a profit, you hope that the emotional and mental benefits of running a business are greater than the daily workload demands.

Clear expectations in your operations provide you a standard, or foundation, on which to stand firm or fall back on, if needed. How you do business tasks, when you perform them, where you perform them, with what measure of excellence you do them all impact your workload. Consistency in operational standards will help your days, weeks, months, and years have some order. The life of a small business owner is never the same from one day to the next. Many people thrive in this type of environment, but operating a small business is not always just innovating, creating, and doing new things. Routine in operations is a vital component of being your own boss. There is a balance between routine and doing something new for the first time for all small business owners. Both are important. New things can exist within routine. Performing with consistency helps you manage your day-to-day operations and also helps your customers trust your business.

Customer Impact

Customers love seeing your creative, one-of-a-kind creations, but they enjoy seeing them in a consistent manner or with some level of order. They like to see consistent pricing schemes—not one product listed in whole dollars and another ending in $0.99. They like to see consistent pictures—not one product that is sharp and clear on a white background and another that is blurry, full of shadows, and has your cat's hair on it. Customers like consistency in shipping—not one product that is shipped the next day and another that is shipped in three weeks.

From the moment customers first view your shop or product, they are forming their expectations of your business. "Will this product meet my needs? Can I trust this seller to provide me with the product in a reasonable quality and time frame?

Will this seller answer my questions in a timely manner? Do the photos and descriptions match my expectations of the product? Can I expect good customer service?"

The customers' expectations are built on your business's individual operational standards. If your operational standards are consistent and good, your customers will feel confident in your business and will be more likely to purchase from you. If your operational standards are inconsistent, they will feel less confident in trusting your business with their purchases.

Etsy sellers want consistent operational standards to run their business. I can't tell you which standards to choose, but I can help you create your own.

Etsy-preneurship Operational Standards

There are eight parts to defining an operational standard. Many great Etsy sellers have these operational standards in place, because they have had the good business sense to enact these instinctively. Other Etsy sellers are operating more by the seat of their pants. Operating by the seat of your pants might work for a while, but it will, most likely, cause burnout or result in having customers who are ultimately not satisfied with the business and decide not make purchases from that shop.

Operational Standards Model

Operational Subject					
Quantity			Quality		
Effectiveness			Efficiency		
Cost			Time		
Clarifying Expectations					
Who	What	Where	When	How	Why

This model is a tool to help you create your own operational standards. The parts that make up the model can help you strengthen your mental muscles for business. For every business operation you perform, you can put that operational subject into this framework to better evaluate options and set clear operational standards or expectations. It is my hope that this model gives you a way to visualize operational standards in a way you have never considered them before. Let's look at each of the eight parts in more detail to help you better understand how you will eventually create your own operational standards for the tasks facing your Etsy business.

Operational Subject

This is the task you perform. It could include topics such as photography, making a product, shipping a product, and even marketing your shop. For each operational task that your business has to perform, you can visualize all the other parts of this model. Every subject will have unique standards of quantity, quality, effectiveness, efficiency, cost, time, and expectations.

Every business will have unique standards relating to each operational task. This uniqueness will eventually set apart the best Etsy shops from the average and mediocre Etsy shops. Let your operations become a competitive advantage.

Quantity

Quantity is the number (amount) of whatever you are measuring. How many photos? How many products? How many Facebook posts? How many views does a product renewal receive? How many days until shipping? How many hours until a convo message is returned? The words "more" and "fewer" are not always appropriate for describing your operations compared to a competitor. Quantity is not just about having the most or least of something (e.g., more free gifts, fewer shipping days). How your competitors answer these questions can possibly influence how you will answer this question. Quantitative issues always have a number tied to them. Sometimes quantity trumps quality; other times, this is not the case.

Quality

Quality is how well something is performed. How awe-inspiring is a photograph? How nice is a product? How viral is a Facebook post? How valuable are individuals' views (do they "heart" your shop instead of just looking at the product for one second)? Does a product arrive damaged or intact when shipped? Did the answer in the convo satisfy their uncertainty? Quality can set your business's operations apart from others, but having the highest quality is not always necessary. Providing a higher quality can often increase your costs. These increased costs have to be passed on to the customer, who might not value that higher level of quality at that price. You must know your customers' expectations while also helping them create their expectations about your business.

Effectiveness

Effectiveness measures whether your operations achieve their goal or whether your actions are adequate to accomplish your purpose. This measure does not look at how you achieve the goal, only *whether* the goal was achieved. For example, consider the operational task of ordering raw materials. You need to buy some thread and fabric, and you know exactly what type you want, so you decide to go to your local craft store to pick it up. Your craft store is 30 minutes away, so you spend 60 minutes in total driving time. You also walk around the store for 45 minutes looking at scrapbook supplies (which are completely unrelated to your small business). Also, when you go to find the fabric, it is not there, so you end up buying only the thread. You then drive an additional 10 minutes to another store to buy the fabric—and it is more expensive than at the first store. You finally make it home, exhausted, and curl up on the coach to read a book and then take a nap.

In this scenario, the task was achieved (purchasing fabric and thread). The operation was effective, but you spent 70 minutes driving, paid too much for the fabric, wasted 45 minutes looking at something unrelated to your business, and ended up wasting another three hours while taking a nap. Effectiveness was achieved, but at the expense of efficiency.

Efficiency

Efficiency means achieving your operational task in the best possible manner while avoiding the waste of time and effort. Etsy sellers should strive for their operations to be both effective and efficient. For example, consider the operational task of taking product photos. One Etsy seller takes photos directly after making each product, and another takes photos directly after making 10 products. The Etsy seller who takes photos of all 10 products at one time is more efficient—setting up the lightbox only once, editing the photos at one time, and "getting in the zone" by taking the pictures one after another. Here's a popular saying to summarize these two related operational measures: "Being effective is about doing the right things, while being efficient is about doing things in the right manner."

Cost

Operational tasks may or may not have direct financial costs tied to them. For example, maybe you take your own product photos with a camera you had already owned as a personal asset; there is no direct financial cost to taking these photos— it is free. But you might realize that your pictures are not very good, so you hire your friend to take the photos for $2 each—now the task has a direct financial cost.

There can also be a financial *opportunity cost* to an operational task. For example, you currently perform all the shipping preparation and mailing for your orders, which takes you an hour a day. Your eight hours of working time each day are jam-packed, and you are selling everything you create. In one hour you can create 10 products that create a profit of $20 each. This means that for every hour you put in creating products, you can create $200 in profit! In a case like this, you should outsource every business-related task that costs less than $200 per hour to perform. Hire your friend to ship the products for you; even if you pay that person $50 an hour to do this, you are still better off with $150 in profit and extra time to do other business-related tasks. Opportunity cost is the loss of gain caused by choosing one alternative over another. Opportunity cost is often related to the value of your time as a small business owner.

Time

There never seems to be enough time in the day for small business owners to accomplish what they want. Time restraints can really impact operations. For example, if you don't make time for communicating with your customers, you will most likely start getting some negative feedback. All operations have to fit into a limited amount of time. This is why scheduling and time management are two of the most important skills for Etsy sellers to learn in order to help their operations run like well-oiled machines. How long should an operational task take you? How long does it actually take you? How can you make it happen in a shorter amount of time? At what time of day are you best able to perform this task? Are there other operational tasks that have a greater priority? How do you manage your operational tasks in relation to time?

Clarifying Expectations (Who, What, Where, When, How, Why)

This is the final and most important part of the creation of your operational standard. The first seven parts were to get your mind thinking about the best way to perform an operational task and how the quantity, quality, effectiveness, efficiency, cost, and time elements can impact your operations. Answering these six questions (who, what, where, when, how, and why) will create your business's operational standard.

Who

Who is going to perform the task? Will you do it, or will someone you hire do it? Can your spouse help you? Do you have a friend who can help you? Do you want to hire an employee or an independent contractor to perform the task? Do you want to pay an online service to help you with the task?

What

What is the operational task? Take the operational subject from the model and expand on it to include the necessary details. For example, your operational subject is "product photography." You now break it down into tasks: Take five photos of the product from five different angles; take pictures when 10 new products are created; use this specific type of background; use these specific camera settings; upload the products into the photo editor software; edit them with three specific embellishments; and save them into a specific file folder with a specific naming convention. This is consistency in action. Consistency allows you to go on semiautomatic pilot and will eventually make you professional at the task you will be performing time after time.

Where

Where will you perform this task? Do you have a designated work area? Do you have a preferred post office? Location creates familiarity.

When

When will you perform the task? Is the task dependent on another task taking place? Is there a certain time of day when you are best able to perform this task? Are there any deadlines that influence when the task is performed (shipping schedules, store hours, or outside lighting for photos)?

How Long

This question is not asking *how* you will perform the task. We defined the "how" in the preceding "what" question. This question is about how long you expect it to take to perform the task. The time element related to this task will help you when you begin using the time management spreadsheet (which you can download at the end of this chapter). How much time does this task require?

Why

This question leads you to know the purpose behind doing an operational task. If ever you don't know why you are doing something, *stop doing it*. In any given business situation, you should always be able to eventually locate the "why" regarding your purpose. The why should also be clearly stated in one of your defining statements (mission, vision, value, competency) that you created in Chapter 1. Look for tasks that can be eliminated. If you perform a task for a while and feel it is not working as you had hoped, feel free to change it.

Example: Operational Standards for Providing Customer Feedback

Here is an example of what the eight-step model looks like for a very routine operational task that Etsy sellers perform when they give feedback to customers who purchased from them. This is an actual operational standard that I use in my JJMFinance Etsy shop. I do this every time I provide feedback, and I go into autopilot mode when performing it, which means I do it really fast.

Operational subject. Providing feedback to Etsy sellers who make a purchase from me.

Quantity. One feedback per purchased item.

Quality. Use my canned feedback message designed for high quality. "Thank you for your purchase. I appreciate your business. I hope this product helps your Etsy shop thrive!" I use the same feedback so I can go fast and do not have to think up something clever to say each time. I think the message is appreciative and sincere. I also include my tagline, "helping your Etsy shop thrive," in the feedback for two reasons. First, I really do hope my product helps them. Second, I hope when customers scan their feedback, they see my message and wonder, "What is that Etsy seller all about?" and click on my shop or product to see what I sell—sincerity with a touch of intrigue.

Effectiveness. This method is effective because I give them positive feedback and accomplish a related goal of creating intrigue through the feedback I give.

Efficiency. This method is efficient, because it takes me 10 seconds to perform immediately after I renew the sold item.

Cost. There is no direct financial cost. The opportunity cost is minimal.

Time. The task takes 10 seconds. I perform it immediately after the purchase to show goodwill and encourage the customer to provide positive feedback to my shop. The task takes place immediately after purchase, if possible.

Clarifying Expectations (Who, What, Where, When, How, Why):

- *Who*? Myself.
- *What*? Provide feedback after renewing the sold item and shipping the product by e-mail; I write the canned feedback message and select a positive feedback rating.
- *Where*? On my laptop at my desk.
- *When*? After renewing the product and shipping it through e-mail.
- *How long*? 10 seconds.
- *Why*? To encourage positive feedback from my customers, market through their feedback, and demonstrate great customer service through timely feedback. This leads to my ultimate business value of *service*.

This might seem like overkill for such a simple operational task, but I am very happy with how it is working. Out of all the sales that my Etsy shop has made, 81.4 percent of these items have received feedback. This is very good, considering the average percentage among the top-performing Etsy sellers is 68 percent, according to my analysis of Etsy's 50 first Quit Your Day Job Sellers. My feedback is also 100 percent positive. I get some really great quotes from customers, which actually encourages potential customers to learn more about my products. I believe my feedback, which is always sincere, will instill confidence in them to purchase my more of my products.

Even though providing feedback is such a simple operational task, I've done this task more than 1,000 times. I don't have to think about it, and it does not distract me from other things.

Operational standards are unique among Etsy sellers. This is the way I perform this task, but it is not the only acceptable way. In fact, you might be thinking, "How can he give the same feedback to everyone? It is so impersonal!" This might be true, but this is how I value feedback for my shop with regard to managing my time and seeking the results I desire. Other Etsy sellers might view the way I give feedback as being inefficient—they may think it is better to save up 10 or 20 feedbacks and perform them all at once through batch feedback. I don't do this, because I value providing a quick feedback reply. The best advice I can offer here is for you to seek out your perfect operational standard, tweak it if it is not working, and stick with it if you like the results.

Setting Your Operational Standards

Following are some of the most common operational standards that Etsy sellers face. For each one of these operational standards, you can go through the eight-step model. You can either write it out or just create the standard in your head. If you need help with the discipline of creating your operational standards, I suggest you write them out, as it will really force you to think about the operation from the different angles; this might help you discover a better way of performing the task. If you already have your own operational standards for each of these topics, it is still worth the exercise of going through them in more detail to see whether you come up with any tweaks to your existing standards.

With all the following operational subjects, there are thousands upon thousands of standards. Just because every Etsy seller has unique standards does not mean that they are all created equal. Read articles, search the Etsy forums, and talk with other Etsy sellers to find what you believe are some of the best standards you can find that match your Etsy shop's purposes. Let these other Etsy shops' standards be a type of benchmark for your own standards. There are lessons to be learned by comparing standards among businesses. We explore some standards on various topics from the Etsy community in Chapter 9.

- *Customer service standards.* What level of customer service do you want to provide to your customers? What does it look like? How do you measure it? What areas of customer service are most important to you? What kind of service do your customers expect from you?

- *Shipping standards.* How will you ship? What days will you ship? With what carrier will you use to ship? How will you price various shipping methods? Will you offer options on shipping? What will you package the products in? Will you ever use insurance? What shipping supplies will you use? Where will you get them? How will you store them?

- *Production standards.* When will you make products? Where will you make them? With what quality will you make them? What designates scraps or a test product? What will you do with imperfect products? How will you ensure consistency among one type of product that you create multiple times? What will the process look like?

- *Raw material standards.* Where will you store the materials? How will you track them? How will you find them easily? How will you know when to reorder? Where will you buy them?

- *Finished inventory standards.* Where will you store them? Will you list all finished inventory? How will you keep them safe? Do you need to insure them? How big will you let your finished inventory grow? How long does a finished inventory item have to be on your shelf before it goes on sale at a reduced price?

- *Photography standards.* What camera will you use? How many photos will you take? How many photos do you want to post per product listing? Where will you take your pictures? What background will you use? How will you create some flow or consistency among photos you take? What camera settings will you use? At what angles will you take the photos?
- *Workplace standards.* How often will you clean your workplace? How messy will you let it get? How organized do you want it to be? Will you let others enter your workplace? Is your workplace comfortable? How will you make your workplace as comfortable as possible? Does your workplace allow for a home office tax deduction (Chapter 4)? How will you organize your workplace (containers and office furniture)? Where will you purchase your office supplies?
- *Listing standards.* How often will you create new listings? How often will you renew a listing? What schedule will you follow for renewing your products? Will

you list new products one at a time, or build them up in batches?

- *Scheduling standards.* When will you create your schedule for the day, week, month? When will you throw your planned schedule out the window? When will you stick to your schedule even if you are unable complete all the tasks you want to complete?
- *Innovation standards.* When will you set apart time to create new products? How will you encourage yourself to think outside the box? What will you look at online to be inspired for new designs?
- *Bookkeeping standards.* When will you perform your bookkeeping? What bookkeeping solution will you use? How will you manage your receipts?
- *Product description standards.* What do you need to always include in your product description? What components of your product descriptions can be the same in all listings? What parts always need to be unique? What links should you include in your product listings?

- *Tagging standards.* How many tags will you use? Will you have some tags that overlap, or are they all unique? Will you create a tagging strategy that tries to achieve depth in a few markets, or will you aim to be wide in many markets?
- *Title standards.* How descriptive will your titles be? Will you use a consistent naming convention? Will you include the best keywords in both the title and tags to reinforce the important keywords?
- *Graphic design standards.* What color scheme will you use? Are all your designs consistent with your brand?
- *Self-development standards.* What books will you read? When will you read them? What tools do you need to do your job? How will you learn new business skills? What are the next steps you need to take to grow as a business owner so that you can grow your business?
- *Feedback standards.* What will your feedback look like? When will you perform it? Will you request sellers to provide feedback if you have not received any from them?

- *Social media standards.* How often will you post? How much time will you give yourself to read other posts? How will you ensure that you don't waste time on social media? How will you measure the effectiveness of your posts?
- *Communication standards.* How long will it take, on average, to answer an e-mail or an Etsy convo? Do you need to write canned responses for frequently asked questions? If you receive a lot of similar questions, should you put the answer in the product description? Should you include a note with all the products you ship? Should you communicate with a customer when you ship an item? How will you communicate with a customer who has not yet paid?
- *Work and life balance standards.* How many hours a day will you work? What hours are off limits to working so that you can value your family time? Will your family have to adjust to your new working schedule? What can you do to make sure your family is not stressed out by your business?

Failing Operational Standards and Correcting the Gap

Operational standards that you create can fail. Despite the thought and purposefulness you put behind an operational standard, it might just not work out. Take the time to evaluate your operational standards to see if any of them are failing or falling behind. The gap is the difference between your expected results (the why) and what is actually being achieved. If the gap is wide, try to correct it, and let your operational standard meet the benchmark of your expected results.

Also, watch out for expectations you have set (who, what, where, when, how, why) changing through time. Maybe you really want to always take five pictures, but you start taking only three. Why the change? Are you running out of time? Do you believe the two extra pictures don't really matter? Are you being lazy? Change happens all the time in a business. Make sure you reflect on whether the change that took place is acceptable and reasonable. No shortcuts!

Download: Productivity Log and Defining Your Operational Standards

Note: To download this document, please go to www.etsy-preneurship.com/downloads.

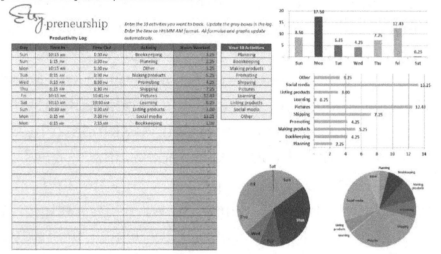

There are two downloads for this chapter. The Productivity Log helps you to track the time you spend and to see how much time you spend on different operational tasks. Use this insight in how you spend your time to see whether you need to spend more time or less time on an operational task—or even to consider whether hiring help is appropriate.

Note: To download this document, please go to www.etsy-preneurship.com/downloads.

 -preneurship

Operational Subject:	Write your operational subject here.
Quantity:	Write your operational subject here.
Quality:	Write your operational subject here.
Effectiveness:	Write your operational subject here.
Efficiency:	Write your operational subject here.
Cost:	Write your operational subject here.
Time:	Write your operational subject here.
Clarifying Expectations	
Who?	Clarify who here. . .
What?	Clarify what here. . .
Where?	Clarify where here . . .
When?	Clarify when here. . .

The second tool helps you define your operational standards using the model we reviewed in this chapter. Define as many operational standards as are appropriate. The operational standard model is meant to help you create consistency; it is a guide to help you think about many different areas affecting your operations that you might not typically think about.

Chapter 8

Marketing

Marketing is one of the core operational tasks that every Etsy seller performs. Etsy sellers who don't perform this task typically go out of business fairly quickly from lack of sales. Sales don't happen magically, and Etsy sellers who just throw a few products up for sale with good intentions to test the waters are doing little more than wasting time. Etsy shops that make consistent sales actively and intentionally market their business, and they do it well.

This chapter does not teach you specific social media techniques, tactics, and strategies. Timothy Adam's book, *How to Make Money Using Etsy: A Guide to the Online Marketplace for Crafts and Handmade Products*, is a great place to learn specific social media skills and applications for your Etsy business. I want to teach you how to run your marketing efforts with efficiency, structure, purpose, and discipline.

No two Etsy sellers use identical marketing methods, and each Etsy seller will gravitate to his or her marketing sweet spot. Some Etsy sellers thrive using only Facebook. Some swear by Pinterest.com to gain sales. Other Etsy sellers hang out in the Etsy forums seeking sales and exposure for their business. Many Etsy sellers use a mix of various marketing methods. This material will help you eventually find your own marketing sweet spot in the following ways:

- You will understand how all marketing activities fall into one of the four parts of the Etsy-preneurship marketing framework.
- You will be able to choose the specific marketing disciplines you want your business to use consistently. (It is better to market well in a few areas than to market poorly in many areas.)
- You will learn how to put these marketing disciplines into action using the 30-day marketing method that can be fully customized to meet your business's specific marketing needs while matching your marketing time restrictions (from five minutes a day to an all-day marketing effort).

Marketing Isn't What It Used to Be

In college textbooks around the world, marketing chapters typically reference the four P's of marketing. The four P's are *price, product, promotion*, and *place*. These four topics are all important when you are thinking about marketing your product. However, if Etsy sellers focused on only these four topics, their Etsy shops would probably fail. Consider this: The *place* is all the same for all Etsy sellers—Etsy. Place is largely irrelevant in this case. Price is important, but if you just list your items and play around by moving the price up and down within a reasonable range, it really does not market your shop and drive sales. Price does not create the type of momentum to produce consistent sales. Products are important, which is why we spent time looking at what type of product to sell in Chapter 2, but there are already hundreds of great products on Etsy created by talented individuals who have mediocre sales numbers. Great products by themselves do not guarantee sales. Products are like cars—they need fuel. Products by themselves have only limited fuel—they need to be filled up with other types of marketing fuel. Last is promotion, or cheering about your product. This is somewhat effective, but if promoting is all you do, your potential customers have promoting amnesia. They forget about you the moment your promotion is not in front of their face. Promoting is useful, but is only part of the Etsy-preneurship marketing framework.

The Etsy-preneurship Practical Marketing Framework

As a small business owner, your marketing needs to be as simple as possible yet still cover all your bases. For large businesses, the marketing department contains many people with various skill sets, specialties, and expertise in various areas of marketing. One person can do only so much, so you always want to make sure you are doing the marketing activities that provide the biggest impact for your effort. I believe that the practical marketing framework important for Etsy sellers consists of four major parts: *branding, connecting, advertising*, and *promotions*. Branding is the most important, followed by connecting, advertising, and promotions (in that order). All types of marketing activities can fit into one of these four parts of marketing.

The Etsy-preneurship marketing framework is all about people and relationships. Each of the four parts of the framework (branding, connecting, advertising, and promotions) has parallels to real-life relational interactions. Branding is your personal identity or your business's brand. Connecting is the interactions and communications with your relationships or with your customers. Advertising is meeting new friends or finding new potential customers. Promotions are inviting friends to participate in activities with you or inviting customers to make purchases or engage in other business-related activities.

Etsy-preneurship Marketing Framework

Promotions

Advertising

Connecting

Branding

Branding

Brand is the identity of your business, which is made up of your name, slogan, colors, feel, tagline, image, tone, design style, literary style, humor, personality, logos, shapes, sound, smell, and taste.

Your shop banner and avatar are part of your brand. Your shop name tells others about your brand. The way you write your product descriptions or welcome customers to your shop in the shop announcement is also a part of your brand. In the end, since your business is most likely owned 100 percent by you, *you* are the brand.

People are naturally drawn to certain people. If people like you, they like the brand "you." If people don't like you, perhaps it's because you are unpleasant or not fun to be around, or you could just be shy. Friendly people make and have friends. Friendly businesses make and have customers. It requires personal effort to make friends, just as it requires marketing effort to have customers. Having *more* friends does not equate to having *better* friends. Would you rather have 10,000 friends or potential customers who collectively buy only a total of three products a month (three sales) or 100 potential customers who each buy three products a month (300 sales)? Pretty much everything you do as a business owner will eventually impact your brand and image. Protecting, developing, and intentionally managing your business' brand should always be on your mind.

Connecting

It isn't worth having people connect with your business if they don't know who and what your business is all about (brand). Connecting is the next step for a branded business to pursue sales in their marketing framework. As a business owner, you will connect with family, friends, other Etsy sellers, potential customers, previous customers, people who don't even know you have a business, and people who are neutral toward you. Social media is the key way Etsy sellers connect with others: through Facebook, Twitter, Pinterest, LinkedIn, blogs, Etsy forums, Etsy teams, e-mail lists, and hundreds of other sites where people connect.

Connections build trust and relationships and sales. These eventually become promoters for your business. Any time you can get people to market your business for you—because they recognize your good work and quality products—you win. They win, too, because they love your business and your products and feel as though they are helping their friends by sharing your business with others.

Advertising

Advertising is like trying to make new friends. You don't make new friends by sitting in your house by yourself. You make friends by going where people are and talking with them. Everyone you talk to won't end up being your friend, but in the act of joining a new club or going to an event you have never been to, you will probably meet some new acquaintances. In the same way, businesses must get their name, product, and brand out among new potential customers in order to make friends; these new friends will then be more likely to purchase from their businesses. Advertising can be any kind of ad, guest blog post, or marketing activity that introduces your business and products to a new audience.

Advertising places you in circles of people or blogs not previously exposed to your work. The moment they first look at your product pictures is similar to the first few seconds of being introduced to a new person. What do they think of you? Are your products something they want to know a little more about? Should they click on the picture to learn more (i.e., ask you some questions and chat with you), or should they just say "Nice to meet you" and leave you and your product behind?

Advertising can lead to the introduction to more people with whom you can connect. And having connections is one of the key ingredients for a successful business.

Promoting

A promotion is where you look to your existing connections to try to get them to take action. Typically, this is to make a purchase or interact positively with your business in some manner. Promotions can include encouraging purchases through the use of coupons, limited-time offers, or buy-one-get-one-free sales (BOGOs); you can even encourage existing connections to join with you via other social media sites to deepen the relationship.

The relational parallel to promoting your business would be asking one of your existing friends to go on a walk with you or to join you for a concert. One individual asks, and the other individual responds. "Will you go for a walk with me tomorrow?" is parallel to your business asking, "Do you want to get a deep discount on the products you love?" All businesses go through various seasons of promoting their products. A business that is *always* promoting becomes stale in the eyes of its customers. If something is always on sale, it isn't on sale—it is just the everyday price. Promotions fill the role of a "holiday" for your business, helping to create excitement and demand for your products.

The Marketing Disciplines

A marketing discipline is something you do to market your business. Each marketing discipline can fall into one or more of the four parts of the marketing framework (branding, connecting, advertising, promoting). Every one of these marketing disciplines can help you build your brand, connect with others, advertise your business, and promote your products. Most Etsy sellers find a handful of marketing disciplines to typically employ for marketing their business. Sometimes an Etsy seller will choose one discipline, find out it is not for them, and then pick up a new discipline. There are hundreds of marketing disciplines, so I won't cover them all here, but I will highlight the 10 most popular among Etsy sellers.

Top 10 Most Popular Etsy Marketing Disciplines

Facebook	Twitter	Pinterest	Etsy	Blogs
Offline marketing	Online (advertising)	E-mail lists	Social bookmarking	Search engine optimization (SEO)

Facebook

Facebook is a social networking website that allows you to create a profile for your business and interact with your business's fans. I highly recommend Facebook as a great way to connect with your customers and potential customers. Facebook gives great flexibility to be creative in how you interact with your fans using pictures, videos, and posts.

Twitter

Twitter is a microblogging social networking service that allows your business the chance to interact with your followers and those you follow through short, 140-character-long tweets (messages). While not as visually appealing as Facebook, it is an easy way to connect with others online.

Pinterest

Pinterest is a virtual pinboard photo-sharing social website. Etsy products make up a good part of what is being shared, and using the site is a great way to let your Etsy products be shared by others through the connections or pins that other people find interesting. Pinterest's growth continues to skyrocket, and I believe it will become more important, impactful, and influential for Etsy sellers in the coming years.

Etsy

Not only is Etsy your storefront, but it is also an active online community that is likely to be interested in your business and products! Etsy teams are groups of Etsy sellers and customers who have common interests or goals and work together to promote each other's products. The Etsy forums are a great place to ask questions, catch up on Etsy news, and build a name for yourself as you interact with other Etsians. Etsy treasuries are a place to feature your own and other Etsy sellers' products in a self-curated collection of 16 product pictures. Some treasuries eventually become the front page of Etsy.com (talk about great exposure!). Etsy search ads are a way to buy keywords that Etsy users are searching. When the keyword comes up, your product will be shown at the top of the search in Etsy's advertisement section. So far, Etsy search ad results have varied with Etsy sellers from being great to a being a bust. I encourage you to at least try it out to see whether it is a good method for your shop.

Blogs

Blogs are virtual journals where you can create posts that talk about anything you want (including your business). Just as no two people write about the same things in their personal journals, no two Etsy sellers have the same content in their blogs. Blogs allow an access point to communicate with your existing friends, colleagues, or clients, and they point potential buyers to a place where they can learn more about your business and products. Blogspot, WordPress, Tumblr, and TypePad are the most popular blog applications used by Etsy sellers.

Offline Marketing

Offline marketing is any type of marketing activity you do that is not online. Typically, most Etsy sellers focus their efforts online, since their storefront is online and their reach is wider. However, there is a place for offline marketing for many Etsy sellers. Offline marketing could include flyers, business cards, posters, sponsoring an event and putting up a banner, wearing your products (if applicable), using an elevator speech with those you meet to tell them about your business, having a friend host a home sale, teaching a class, placing advertisements in newsletters or magazines, and hundreds of other personal marketing endeavors. Before the Internet, these were the only marketing disciplines available, so I call these *traditional* marketing disciplines.

Online (Advertisements)

You've already considered what type of websites your customers visit in the customer profile section of your business plan (Chapter 2); advertising on these websites is an easy way to reach out to your current and future customers. I've seen this question asked so many times in the Etsy forums: "What are the best websites to advertise your business?" There is no answer to this question. You must find it yourself, and this does cost money and requires trial and error. You might advertise on one website and get very few clicks, while another website might produce lots of clicks for you. You should always consider the *cost per click*, and remember, the quality of the click is also important. Compare among websites to find which cost per click and quality of click gives you the biggest bang for your purchase. Also, remember that if you find a really good place to advertise, it is somewhat rare. Don't expect to hear about it in the Etsy forums. A good online advertisement is worth a lot for the exposure it provides for your Etsy business.

E-mail Lists

Having your customer sign up to be included in an e-mail list is a great way to communicate specific messages and promotions with your connections. E-mail lists have some of the highest response rates among marketing disciplines. A few of the more popular services to manage e-mail lists include AWeber, MailChimp, and Constant Contact. Remember, e-mail your customers only if they asked to be included in the lists. E-mailing previous customers over and over without their permission is a good way to lose influence with them.

Social Bookmarking

Social bookmarking is a way to organize bookmarks of online resources and organize, store, and manage them with tags or labels. The most popular social bookmarking sites include StumbleUpon, Delicious, Reddit, and Digg.

Search Engine Optimization (SEO)

I believe this marketing discipline is a must for every Etsy seller. It is a way to improve how your products, shop, and websites come up in search results. Search engine optimization is involved in how you title and tag your products on Etsy (Etsy SEO). Google also uses SEO to interpret your products in its search engine. Google and Etsy SEO can work together. Effective keywords are the essence of good SEO marketing. SEO is part art and part science. In Chapter 9, I refer you to some good resources to learn how to perform SEO properly.

Marketing Strategies Need Structure

Now that you know the four main parts of marketing (branding, connecting, advertising, and promoting) and are aware of the 10 most popular marketing disciplines (Facebook, Twitter, Pinterest, Etsy, blogs, offline marketing, online advertising, e-mail lists, social bookmarking, and SEO), what do you do next? Unfortunately, many Etsy sellers try to do it all with no strategy or structure; some just don't know where to start because of feelings of being overwhelmed. If you go on a journey without a destination or a map, there is a good chance that you won't be fully happy with where you end up and how you got there. The same idea applies to your Etsy shop's marketing strategy. If you try to do all the marketing disciplines, or if you have no goals about your marketing purposes, you will probably have results that match—few connections and few sales.

When it comes to marketing your Etsy shop, intentionality is important. You need to know what you want to accomplish from your marketing activities. You also don't have all the time in the world to market your shop; you are on a time budget. You need to have realistic expectations for how long you will market each day. You also need help to follow your planned marketing activities. It is easy to forget what you should do, when you should do it, and how you should do it.

I've found that the best solution to meet these demands is a 30-day marketing method.

The 30-Day Etsy-preneurship Marketing Plan

The 30-Day Etsy-preneurship marketing method will help you set clear objectives for your marketing, give you focus in your daily tasks, and help you stay on track during the month. The download at the end of this chapter is the 30-Day Etsy-preneurship marketing plan. However, before we start using the tool, let's learn a little more about the marketing plan.

What Does It Look Like?

Every 30 days, you will create or modify your existing marketing plan. First, you will state goals for branding, connecting, advertising, and promoting. Next, you will choose the disciplines you want to focus on that month. After that, you will determine how much time you can spend per day on marketing activities. Last, you will specify specific marketing activities that you will do each day. After following these four steps, you will have your 30-day marketing plan to follow. During the month, you just have to reference your marketing plan and perform the activity. Once you perform the activity, you can update the spreadsheet to mark it complete and/or add any relevant notes.

How Much Time Does It Take?

Etsy sellers all have different amounts of time to spend on marketing their Etsy business. I know of some Etsy sellers who spend five minutes a day marketing their Etsy business and others who spend several hours. For sellers whose Etsy shop is part of their full-time job, you would expect more time to be spent marketing. If you have five minutes a day available, market for five minutes a day. If you have one hour a day, market one hour a day. If you have a packed Wednesday, don't market on Wednesdays. That is one of the benefits of the 30-day marketing planner: It is fully customizable to your needs and schedule.

I suggest most Etsy sellers should market a minimum of 15 minutes a day and no more than three hours a day. Each time you use the 30-day method, you can tweak the time you need to market. If you are not happy with the number of sales and connections you made during a month, you can increase the time that you spend on marketing. If you begin to find smarter ways to market your shop (becoming more efficient), you can begin to cut down on the amount of time you market your business.

Budgeting your time is also useful for when you are first beginning your business's marketing plan. For example, you might not have a Facebook or Twitter account, but you want to market using these sites. You can easily budget larger blocks of time to start setting up and creating your Facebook and Twitter accounts during the month. Maybe you don't know much about Pinterest. In this case, you could also budget time to create your Pinterest account and schedule time to read some websites and books about using Pinterest to market your products.

Promotesy.com is a website that allows Etsy sellers to automate their marketing plan in advance by scheduling tweets, Facebook posts, and other social media marketing efforts. This service complements the 30-day marketing plan.

Why 30 Days?

I believe that 30 days (or one month) is the perfect amount of time to start planning your upcoming marketing activities. Every month, you should be updating your bookkeeping and finding out how many sales and the amount of profit you make. You can easily compare the amount of sales and profit you made to the marketing activities that you performed. Over time, you should be able to see a correlation between the marketing activities you perform during the month and the amount of sales you receive.

Thirty days is a manageable time frame. It is long enough that you can set goals and have time to begin achieving them. It is also short enough that you can find out quickly what works and what does not work in marketing your shop. Remember, marketing your shop will take time to build some momentum, so don't quit after a few months of not seeing the type of results you are looking for.

An Example: The 30-Day Etsy-preneurship Marketing Plan

This example is to give you an idea of what a 30-day marketing plan might look like for an Etsy shop that has been marketing for a few months.

The first part is setting clear goals by performing the four objectives of marketing:

1. *Branding goal.* Write three blog posts that tell about my work studio, my mission statement, and a funny crafting story. Update my Facebook page to include product pictures that strengthen my brand using my business color scheme. Update my shop policies to sound more professional.

2. Connecting goal. Connect with my fans on Facebook and Twitter, sharing products and a blog feature on my new jewelry line. Ask three questions to my Facebook fans to encourage interaction. Start up my Pinterest account and learn how to use it for marketing purposes while creating 10 unique pinboards. Gain 25 more likes on Facebook. Follow 25 more individuals on Twitter.

3. Advertising goal. Find a website on which to advertise for two weeks that costs $30 or less with an expectation of 120 clicks. Join a new Etsy team and meet some new individuals.

4. Promoting goal. Send an e-mail to my entire e-mail list and offer them a coupon for 20 percent off and a free gift if they order during a one-week period. Promote this sales event on Facebook, Twitter, and Pinterest. Promote three products for the Easter holiday this month.

Next, you will clearly define the marketing disciplines you will use during the next 30 days. Don't try to overdo it here. As you gain more marketing experience, this list will become more diverse.

- Marketing disciplines: Blog, Facebook, Twitter, Pinterest, e-mail list, online advertising.

Then you will set your time schedule for the next 30 days.

- Time: I will market for 20 minutes a day. Every Wednesday, I will not market at all due to a busy schedule. I will set aside one hour for creating a Pinterest account and three hours for learning how to use it.

Last, you will create your 30-day marketing plan.

Day 1: 20 minutes; write and post blog article about my workspace; share on Facebook and Twitter.

Day 2: No marketing.

Day 3: 20 minutes; buy advertising for two-week advertisement.

Day 4: 20 minutes; two-week online advertisement begins; promote Easter holiday product 1 on Facebook.

Day 5: One hour; set up Pinterest account; promote Easter holiday product 1 on Twitter.

Day 6: 20 minutes; write and post blog article about my mission statement; share on Facebook and Twitter.

Day 7: 20 minutes; ask question about crafting hobbies to Facebook fans; find 10 new people to follow on Twitter.

Day 8: Two hours; learn about marketing using Pinterest at Handmadeology.com.

Day 9: No marketing.

Day 10: One hour; read e-book about Pinterest marketing techniques.

Day 11: 20 minutes; join new Etsy team and post in five of the forum posts; promote Easter holiday product 2 on Facebook and Twitter.

Day 12: 20 minutes; promote Easter holiday product 3 on Facebook and Twitter; pin it on Pinterest.

Day 13: 20 minutes; send promotional e-mail to e-mail list offering 20 percent coupon; share about the coupon on Facebook and Twitter.

Day 14: 20 minutes; update Facebook landing page to include pictures of my products that match my business's color scheme.

Day 15: 20 minutes; ask question to Facebook fans about favorite Easter colors; promote 1 product on Facebook and Twitter.

Day 16: No marketing.

Day 17: 20 minutes; write and post blog article on funny craft story; share and post on Facebook and Twitter.

Day 18: 20 minutes; two-week online advertisement ends; measure advertisement results (clicks, cost per click, impact).

Day 19: 20 minutes; post on Facebook and Twitter a reminder about the 20 percent coupon.

Day 20: 20 minutes; retweet (RT) another Etsy seller's promotional tweet; repost one of your previously posted blog articles.

Day 21: 20 minutes; find two blog posts that are not my own that I believe my fans might enjoy, and post on Facebook.

Day 22: 20 minutes; update my shop policies to sound more professional.

Day 23: No marketing.

Day 24: 20 minutes; find five more people to follow on Twitter; retweet two messages that I like.

Day 25: 20 minutes; ask question to Facebook fans about what product of mine they want to see in their Easter basket this year.

Day 26: 20 minutes; create five pinboards on Pinterest.

Day 27: 20 minutes; post a product on Facebook that I just created and tell a short message about why I created it.

Day 28: 20 minutes; post a joke on Twitter relating to my craft.

Day 29: 20 minutes; create five pinboards on Pinterest; find 10 more people to follow on Twitter; post a shop section on my Facebook page and share about why it is my favorite.

Day 30: No marketing.

Free and Low-Cost Marketing Methods for Etsy Sellers

In no particular order, here are dozens of free and low-cost marketing methods that can benefit Etsy sellers immensely: using Twitter, treasuries, Flickr, Etsy forums, blogs, and Facebook, taking better photos, linking in your product descriptions to other parts of your Etsy shop, using promo coupon codes, handing out business cards, commenting on other blogs, commenting in Etsy's blog, giving away products, using all your tags, sending out newsletters, using Etsy's circles, "hearting" products you like, leaving feedback, updating your Etsy location so people can find you, shopping local, using financial checks with photos of your products and business, offering international shipping, giving free gifts and business cards to customers, offering free trials, listing your site in online directories, creating a web page, using Pinterest, collaborating on products with other Etsy sellers, using Kaboodle, wearing your product, posting flyers in your local community, donating items to charity, teaching a free class, mailing postcard ads, promotions in conjunction with other Etsy sellers, joining a promotional Etsy team, exchanging business cards with other Etsy sellers, making use of StumbleUpon, LinkedIn, Squidoo, Craftgawker, Tumblr, and e-mail lists, selling at craft fairs, looking for marketing services at fiverr.com, making YouTube videos, exchanging advertising on other Etsy sellers' blogs, guest-writing blog articles, using Etsy search ads, offering business brand product giveaways (notepads, pencils, etc.), using free classifieds, selling on Craigslist, bookmarking libraries or giveaways, using buttons, using word of mouth, offering car magnets, bumper stickers, or T-shirts with your logo, sending Happy Birthday cards to customers, offering product brochures, sending thank-you letters with coupons enclosed, creating crafting parties to sell your products, giving your products as gifts to friends and family, using <u>Tophatter.com</u>, using Google AdWords, writing PR articles for local paper, going on local radio as a guest, joining a local small business group, advertising on Facebook, using an e-mail signature, adding/claiming your business on Google, using viral videos or Internet memes, advertising on Project Wonderful.

Good Product Photos Sell: 10 Tips to Make Etsy's Front Page

Having good product photos is one of the most important aspects of helping your marketing efforts take off. If you have horrible pictures of your products, it doesn't matter how much you market your items, they will rarely sell. Good pictures sell. One of the best places to see what type of pictures are gaining the most views and traffic is to look at the types of photos that are shown on Etsy's front page. Many Etsy sellers who have made the front page remember the first time that happened and were excited by the exposure it brought to their shop. I've seen sales spike and views skyrocket in many shops that make the front page.

It is useful to just look at the pictures and see what types of pictures are making the front page, but I wanted to see something statistical or scientific to try to find out what type of products have the best chance of making the front page. This is why I designed an experiment, which I call "The Naked Truth about Making Etsy's Front Page." In this experiment, I observed 112 different front-page pictures and gathered 10 pieces of data about each picture.

After running the experiment, crunching the numbers, and analyzing the data, this is my conclusion: To statistically increase the likelihood of having products make the front page of Etsy, you should use a white background; list a product in the art, jewelry, or vintage Etsy category; center your product in the picture; take the picture of the whole product; don't use a human model in the picture; let the product be the only thing in the picture; take the picture straight on; keep the background and picture simple; don't perform any noticeable modifications to the picture; and don't use any letter embellishments.

This conclusion is not a magical formula, and obviously pictures make the front page all the time that don't follow these guidelines. But numbers don't lie, and this is the profile of product pictures that most often make Etsy's front page. These statistics can help you run your business better and help your business grow.

Download: The 30-Day Marketing Method

Note: To download this document, please go to www.etsy-preneurship.com/downloads.

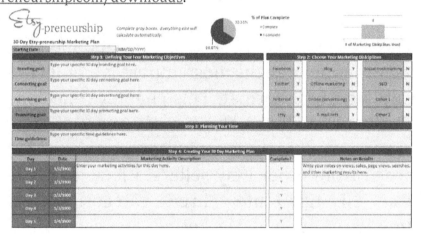

Use this tool to develop your 30-day marketing plan initially; use it daily to implement your plan; then evaluate the plan's success at the end of the 30-day period. Keep tweaking your plan every 30 days to improve the results, and never let your marketing efforts become stagnant.

Chapter 9

Etsy Community

40 Etsy Tips, Tricks, and Nuggets

Since the moment I first started selling on Etsy, I have relied on other Etsy sellers' experience, wisdom, trial and error, and helpfulness to improve my business. The Etsy community is the source of these tips, tricks, and nuggets, and I have tried to summarize the most important topics in an easily digestible format. This chapter reflects the collective knowledge of my many years of selling on Etsy, as well as the most important things I have learned from other Etsy sellers. I have organized these 40 tips into three categories: Etsy, Administration, and Marketing. For each topic, I share some of the intricacies and nuances that I believe will help your Etsy shop thrive!

How to Implement Tips, Tricks, and Nuggets

For each topic, I share knowledge that comes from my personal experience, tips I have read in the

Etsy forums shared by other Etsy sellers, tricks of the trade that Etsy sellers have learned through experience, and nuggets of wisdom that the most successful Etsy sellers have shared through the Etsy forums and blogs. Many of these topics can take days, weeks, or years to master, so this chapter serves as an introduction in your small business adventure on Etsy. For each topic, I have put together a "Must-Read Etsy Articles (Top 100)" that can be downloaded at Etsy-preneurship.com. Consider this list your reading assignment after reading this book. I highly recommend you read these articles and the related blog comments. They will really narrow your focus and help you become proficient in these areas of running a small business. Here are the steps I recommend you follow as you attempt to implement these tips, tricks, and nuggets into your Etsy business.

1. Read the entire chapter to get an understanding of the topics and the basic ideas you can easily implement into your Etsy shop immediately.

2. Write down the five topics that interest you most and that you want to learn more about.

3. Download the "Must-Read Etsy Articles (Top 100)" list from Etsy-preneurship.com.

4. Read the articles related to the five topics you chose, and begin implementing these in your business.

5. Repeat this process until you have a more successful Etsy business!

Etsy Tips, Tricks, and Nuggets

Running a business on Etsy is generally very easy, but you need to know your way around the site, your Etsy shop, and the tools it offers to help make your selling experience go smoothly. Etsy is constantly adding new features, taking away things that don't work as it had hoped, and generally trying to make the site the best possible experience for both sellers and customers. Here are the Etsy-specific tips, tricks, and nuggets to help you become comfortable selling on Etsy and run a smooth operation.

1. Etsy Shop Statistics

Etsy provides statistics about your Etsy shop's performance. Some of these statistics include tracking views, favorites, orders, revenue, traffic sources (off Etsy), traffic sources (on Etsy), keywords used by customers to find your shop, page views, listing favorites, and search ads statistics. These statistics can be shown for any time period you desire (month, year, or specific date range). These statistics are extremely valuable to evaluate the effectiveness of your Etsy business. Is traffic up or down? Did that promotional campaign increase your traffic and sales orders? Which keywords are working for your products, and which ones are ignored? What trends do you see and where do you hope for them to be in the future? I suggest you check your shop stats at least weekly, but following it once a day allows you to have greater insight into the day-to-day traffic of your Etsy shop. Don't fall into the time waster of checking your Etsy stats every 20 minutes, as it won't help drive traffic and sales for your business. Look at the graphs to see visualization of the four main categories (views, favorites, orders, and revenue). Etsy shop statistics can be found by clicking on the "your shop" link at the top right of the Etsy homepage and then "shop stats."

Something of interest that I like to look at on Etsy is what I call "reading the views gap." I typically pull up the views graph for the past month and look at the relationship between the blue line (shop views) and purple line (listing views). If your purple line is above your blue line, you know that customers who land on your shop page typically look at more than one product. If your blue line is above your purple line, you know that customers are looking at individual products more than your shop. I also look at how wide the space is between the two lines. Is it consistent? What causes it to vary based upon your promotional efforts? Find your most successful selling day on Etsy, see which line is higher or lower, and note the width of the gap. Try re-creating this to see if you get the same sales results. This is one type of technical analysis that can help your Etsy shop get more sales.

2. Etsy Shop Announcements

Etsy shop announcements, which show up directly beneath your shop's banner, are a good way to communicate with customers or welcome them to your Etsy shop. Only a few sentences show up automatically, and Etsy requires the reader to click "read more" to read the entire announcement. This makes the first few sentences of your announcements more important than the last words you share. Some common things that are included in shop announcements include a welcome, a little about yourself, something personal, a sales announcement or coupon code, the mission of your business, positive feedback from other customers, encouraging convos, most important shop policies, encouraging customers to look at specific listings, telling where you shop has been featured recently (blogs, TV, magazines), other related website links, sharing about Etsy teams, or anything else you think your customers need to know. Change your shop announcements every once in a while so your welcome does not become stale, or stick with an announcement you know that works well. Etsy shop announcements can be found by clicking on the "your shop" link at the top right of the Etsy homepage and then "info & appearance."

I suggest you word the first few sentences of your announcements carefully and see what shows up on your shop's homepage. The goal is to tell your site's visitors something important while also leaving them wanting to know more. This will give them every encouragement to click on "read more" to finish reading. Maybe you could have an announcement that reads, "MyEtsyShopName is YourTaglineHere—providing product A, product B, and product C. Check out our clearance section. Something amazing happened last month when . . . read more." If customers read your announcement, they really want to click on "read more" to find out what happened that was so amazing. When customers engage with your announcement, they get to know you more and spend more time in your shop. Time builds trust, and trust invariably helps lead to sales.

3. Etsy E-mail Lists

Etsy can send valuable communication and e-mail to you if you opt in. Receiving Etsy e-mails is helpful for staying up-to-date with what is happening overall on Etsy. You can get e-mails when customers send you a convo or add you to their circle and tell you about new features on the site. Shopping guides that can show you the hottest trends may be found on Etsy, international Etsy market news, and in several newsletters (Etsy News, Etsy Teams, Etsy Success, and Etsy Labs). I think every Etsy seller should sign up for all the newsletters, as these publications are specific for Etsy sellers and have helpful, timely tips. Etsy e-mail lists can be found by clicking on the "your account" link at the top right of the Etsy homepage, then "settings," followed by the "e-mails" tab.

I suggest you sign up for anything you are remotely interested in; it is easy to ignore an e-mail, but you might miss something important if you choose not to receive the message. Etsy Success is so valuable for Etsy sellers and contains tips similar to those in this chapter and book. I read every Etsy Success article when it comes out, because they are so helpful!

4. Etsy Shop Suspension

Although it is rare, an Etsy shop can be suspended for various reasons (typically, for some variation of not following Etsy's rules). First, make sure you read Etsy's "Do's and Don'ts," located at www.etsy.com/help/article/483, to make sure you are following the rules. Second, make sure you are prepared if this ever happens to you, which means having a viable plan of action to remedy the situation. Third, some actions on your part can serve as insurance to your business if this ever happens to you: Save your product photos; have an alternative site to sell from; save your product descriptions; keep positive feedback from customers; have copies of your banner and avatar; and save some screenshots of your Etsy Shop Stats to remember top-performing keywords). There is a list of alternative selling venues and my commentary on each site on the Chapter 9 web page of Etsy-preneurship.com.

5. Etsy Forums

The Etsy forums are a place for the Etsy community to talk, ask questions, and share advice. Forum sections include From the News Blog, Announcements, Site Help, Business Topics, Ideas, and Bugs. I look at the forum headlines almost daily, just to keep a pulse on what the hot topics are in the Etsy community. Although promotion is not supposed to happen in the forums, many Etsy sellers claim that they receive sales as a result of participating in the forums. Based on what I've heard from various Etsy sellers, this is because participation in the forums creates visibility for sellers, which can lead to sellers perusing each other's respective Etsy sites. This, of course, could possibly lead to sales. I don't suggest you use the forums as a method to gain sales, but rather as a way to interact with other Etsy sellers and learn additional tips, tricks, and nuggets. The Business Topics and Announcements from Etsy Admin are the most helpful for a small business owner. The Etsy forums can be found by clicking on the "community" link at the top left of the Etsy homepage and then "forums."

6. Etsy Featured Items

As a shop owner, Etsy allows you to place four products of your choice at the top of your shop page, right below your shop announcement. I suggest that these four products showcase your best pictures and most popular sellers. I believe it is important to highlight a range of prices in this area so that customers know they may purchase something from you that won't break their wallet. Your shop's featured items can be accessed by clicking on the "your account" link at the top right of the Etsy homepage and then clicking the star under the feature column. The star will turn green when a product will be considered for being featured in your Etsy shop. After selecting these green stars, you can manage the order in which they appear on the "featured" tab on the same page.

7. Etsy Bill

When you list products, make sales, and purchase advertising on Etsy, you will be charged for your activity in an "Etsy Bill." I suggest you pay your Etsy bill once each month. The best time to do so is when you are performing your bookkeeping. I suggest you consistently pay either the total balance or the amount due. Some Etsy sellers prefer paying via PayPal to keep documentation of the transaction in PayPal. I prefer paying with a credit card to earn related credit card points.

Glance at your Etsy bill to make sure you have not been charged for anything that you should not have been charged for. You can also analyze what part of your Etsy bill is related to sales, listing new items, and renewing items. The Etsy bill can be found by clicking on the "your shop" link at the top right of the Etsy homepage and then "Your Bill." You can also download a CSV file of your monthly bills by clicking on the hyperlink of a particular month's bill, then clicking on the "Download this entire monthly statement as a CSV file" link at the bottom of the monthly details.

8. Etsy Shop Banner

The Etsy shop banner is one of the first things customers will see in your shop; it will help distinguish your brand, and it should look professional. Many Etsy sellers create their own banner using Paint.NET or Adobe Photoshop. If you lack the skills to make a professional banner, I suggest you find an Etsy seller who can do this for you. I like shop banners that show the product, tell you something about the brand, and might include the shop name and tagline. Banners that are unprofessional make me want to stop looking at a shop almost immediately. If other customers feel this way, this could mean a loss of sales for a potentially good product because it has an ineffective banner. Shop banners can be uploaded by clicking on the "your shop" link at the top right of the Etsy homepage and then "Info & Appearance."

9. Etsy Shop Profile Picture

The Etsy shop profile picture (formerly called an avatar) is visible to customers when they are visiting your shop. The picture is shown on the left sidebar as well as when you make comments in the Etsy forums. Most Etsy sellers have headshots of themselves, their products, or their brand logo as their picture. Again, if you cannot create a professional-looking profile picture, find an Etsy seller to make one of these for you. The Etsy shop profile picture can be edited by clicking on the "your account" link at the top right of the Etsy homepage and then "public profile."

10. Etsy Shop Policies

The Etsy shop policies are where you can tell your potential customers details about your transaction. Not every customer will read your shop policies, so I encourage you to put key elements of your shop policies in your product description. Etsy allows you to provide a welcome message, payment policy, shipping policy, refund policy, additional information, and any other seller information you want to include. I have found that the simpler the policy is, the easier it is for customers to remember it. A simple policy is also easier for you to fulfill.

One of the easiest ways to create your own shop policies is to look at the policies of other Etsy shops and pick and choose policies that work best for your situation. Policies should be fair for both the customer and yourself. Focus on policies that are clear, precise, and simple. I also suggest you keep a hard copy of your policies written in a word processing document for safekeeping. The Etsy shop policies can be edited by clicking on the "your shop" link at the top right of the Etsy homepage, then on "Info & Appearance," then on the "policies" tab.

11. Etsy Treasuries

Etsy treasuries are curated lists of 16 products put together by Etsy sellers and customers. Many Etsy customers and sellers use these treasuries as promotional tools to gain views, exposures, and clicks for their products. There are no hard-and-fast rules for creating a treasury, but Etsy has given guidance regarding which type of treasuries it is most likely to consider using on the front page of Etsy. Treasuries allow you to be creative with other people's Etsy products. Some Etsy sellers complain that certain sellers land on the front page of Etsy repeatedly. I have done a study that showed that the Etsy sellers who are more frequently on the front page happen to be in more treasuries. They are in more treasuries because they typically have really good photos. There is also a correlation between the number of front-page appearances a shop has made and the number of sales it has made. Better pictures lead to more treasuries. More treasuries lead to more exposure. More exposure leads to more sales. Etsy treasuries can be located by finding the Treasury hyperlink on the left sidebar of the Etsy homepage.

12. Etsy Profile (About)

The Etsy shop profile is an easy place for potential customers to learn more about you as an artist or small business owner. I think the best profiles tell a little about the business, how the business came into being, and some interesting bits of information about the seller. Don't write a novel! You can edit your Etsy profile (or "about" page) by clicking on the "your account" link in the top right corner of the Etsy homepage and then on "public profile."

13. Etsy Shop Categories

Etsy allows your products to be classified into a maximum of 10 shop categories. I suggest you use these categories to the fullest of your capacity. I once did a study of some of the most successful Etsy sellers and found a direct correlation between the number of sections a shop has and the number of sales it has. The more products you have to sell, the more likely you are to have a lot of sales, thus the easier it is for the customer to find those products and the more likely a customer is to make a purchase.

Possible category types include product lines, product types, design styles, colors, sizes, and prices. I find that many Etsy customers eventually shop by categories when they find a shop they really like. Some shop owners prefer to use all capital letters, all lowercase, or mixed cases. Just make sure your categories are also good keywords, as these will help in all searches. You can create and edit your shop sections by clicking on the "your shop" link in the top right corner of Etsy's homepage, then on "sections" on the left toolbar.

14. Etsy Product Descriptions

The write-up that accompanies every Etsy product can either finalize a sale or make it fall apart. Product descriptions should not be distracting. They should be clear, concise, answer a customer's questions, and build trust for the transaction to take place. The use of bullets and short sentences is beneficial in aiding readability. Make sure there are no spelling or grammar errors, as these can cause some people to lose trust in the professionalism of your business and product quality. Some Etsy sellers use product descriptions as a time to sell their brand through creative writing. This is helpful for certain types of products, but don't get carried away—this is a product description, not a creative short story. Product descriptions can be created during the product listing steps found by clicking on the "your shop" link, then "add new item."

15. Renewing Products on Etsy

Renewing a product costs an additional listing fee, but it helps your product appear fresh. Etsy's search used to be influenced most by the recentness of a product listing. This made renewing products of utmost importance. Now that Etsy's search is more heavily influenced by relevancy, this, to some extent, diminishes the importance of renewing products on Etsy. Most successful Etsy sellers still have a renewing strategy that they follow to help their listings appear fresh and active to both their customers and Etsy. I have never heard of a one-size-fits-all strategy that is the magic formula. Some renew monthly, others daily, and some never renew unless an item expires or sells. Find something that works for your business and stick with it. You can renew products by clicking on the "your shop" link in the top right-hand corner of the Etsy homepage, then selecting the checkboxes for the products you want to renew and clicking the word "renew."

16. Etsy Search Ads

Etsy released Etsy Search Ads for the first time in September 2011. This allows Etsy sellers to set an advertising budget to purchase impressions that show up when certain keywords are searched by Etsy customers. An *impression* is when an ad shows up on the computer screen of potential customers—they might view it briefly, simply ignore it, or (you hope) click on it. Overall, some Etsy sellers have seen this to be a useful tool, whereas others have claimed no sales accrue from the advertising purchases. I suggest you test it out a few times and form your own conclusion about the usefulness of this advertising method for your small business. Search ads can be created by clicking on the "your shop" link in the top right-hand corner of the Etsy homepage and then clicking on "search ads" on the left sidebar.

17. Etsy Conversations (Convos)

Convos are the way that Etsy sellers communicate with their customers and other Etsy sellers. Some customers are not aware that they can communicate through Etsy's messaging system, so you will have to connect with them through e-mail or other means. If you find yourself providing similar answers to multiple customers, you might consider including that information in the product description or creating a canned response that you can just copy and paste to answer their questions. Conversations can be reached by clicking on the envelope icon at the top of any Etsy page.

18. Etsy Relevancy Search

The Etsy Relevancy Search is the formula or method from which Etsy showcases certain products after a customer types a particular keyword in the search box. Mastering the Etsy

Relevancy Search takes time to research and understand. It also takes time, knowledge, and the correct tools to implement, but it is worth knowing inside and out; the ability to get your products to the top of an Etsy customer's search is worth its weight in gold. Customers often find what they are looking to purchase very soon after they perform a search, and you want your product to be at the top of that list, not at the bottom of the list on page 100.

While no one knows the exact algorithm or formula for Etsy's search ranking criteria, Etsy has revealed some information. Titles are the most important (especially the words at the front of a title). Recentness or how soon it was listed or renewed is second. The third most important thing to focus on is tags. With this high-level understanding of its search ranking criteria, I believe there are five unique strategies Etsy sellers can employ to take full advantage of their titles and tags. Titles and tags should work together to accomplish your search strategy. Titles and tags in your Etsy shop can be either deep or wide.

If your titles and tags are *deep*, it means that you use keywords or phrases multiple times in many of your products in the hope that when potential customers type in these words, many of your products will show up in the results to help them find your shop. Deep relevancy can be viewed as intentionally duplicating titles and tags. With deep titles and tags, you are better represented when someone searches that specific word or phrase.

If your titles and tags are *wide*, it means that you use a variety of keywords or phrases once in your products in the hope that you spread your net wide. This will help potential customers find your shop with the wide variety of keywords they use to search. Wide relevancy can be viewed as intentionally using many different types of words and phrases that describe your products. With wide titles and tags, you are represented at least once with a customer's search, but will show up only once, not many times, within that search.

From this concept of deep versus wide tags, there are five specific title-and-tag strategies you can employ in your Etsy shop. I developed the following five strategies soon after Etsy launched the relevancy-based search. I have subsequently heard fantastic feedback from Etsy sellers who have employed these strategies intentionally, many of whom have gone from almost the bottom of the search to the top of the search. No one strategy is better than another, but each strategy should be chosen intentionally. Here are the five relevancy search strategies:

1. *Superdeep*. Titles deep. Tags deep. This is for Etsy sellers who are very confident in the words that their customers use to search. They have a good feel for the variety of phrases that will be used and are confident that they will be searched in the future. They want to be well represented in these searches.

2. *Moderately deep*. Titles deep. Tags wide. This is for Etsy sellers who are more confident than most that they know what their customers are searching by going deep with their titles (higher rating in the Etsy Relevancy algorithm); they also desire to have their products seen by a wider audience through wide tags.

3. *Middle ground*. Titles mixed. Tags mixed. This is for Etsy sellers who desire to show up in some specific searches and also to spread the net wide for both titles and tags. With this strategy, you get the best of both worlds, but at the expense of some deeper and wider searches.

4. *Moderately wide*. Titles wide. Tags deep. This is for Etsy sellers who want to reach the widest audience possible via their titles and yet go deep through tags. They are less confident than most that they know what their customers are typing in as keywords, or they desire their products to be seen by the most people, not just those with specific search words or phrases.

5. *Superwide*. Titles wide. Tags wide. This is for Etsy sellers who want the greatest amount of people to see their products and who desire very little repetition in keywords or phrases in both tags and titles. These titles and tags are unique for all their products.

These concepts just scratch the surface of the research and work you will need to do in order to perform well in the Etsy searches. Concepts used in search engine optimization (SEO) are also very helpful in getting your Etsy products to the top of the searches on Etsy.

19. Etsy Circles

Etsy circles are a way for Etsy sellers to share their style and favorite items on Etsy with others. Having many circles shows that you have an influence on others in the style and type of products you like. Circles, however, are not a promotional method in and of themselves. Some Etsy sellers are confused by circles, but I view them as a neutral feature on Etsy. From my perspective, circles do not subtract or add much value. You can find your Etsy circles by looking at your Etsy shop's homepage and clicking the word "circles" on the left sidebar.

20. Etsy Seller Handbook

The *Etsy Seller Handbook* is a blog put together by Etsy that covers new Etsy-related tips, tricks, and nuggets. It is must-read material! You can find the *Etsy Seller Handbook* by clicking the word "blog" on the top left of the Etsy homepage and then clicking "Etsy Seller Handbook."

21. Etsy Feedback

You receive feedback from those who purchase your products. Having positive feedback gives your customers greater trust in your business's operations. If you have enough transactions, you will eventually receive neutral or negative feedback that you think you did not deserve—this is just one of those things that happens while selling on Etsy. Don't let it get you down, but continue to do your best to have excellent customer service. Try to make the situation right by using Etsy's "Kiss and Makeup" feature to turn that unflattering feedback into something positive. Sadly, not all customers will understand this feature and will ignore your attempts to make things right. Unfortunately, with this in mind, I guess sometimes a customer likes to leave unhappy. Etsy's feedback system might not be perfect, but it serves its purpose. You can view your feedback by clicking on "your account" in the top right-hand corner of Etsy's homepage and then clicking on "feedback."

22. Etsy Teams

Etsy teams are one of the best ways to connect and meet other Etsy sellers and customers. I suggest all Etsy sellers find a few teams that they like and participate and encourage one another. There are thousands of unique Etsy teams; some have thousands of members, others just a few. Some teams are very active, and others are ghost towns. Some teams have requirements to join, and others are merely social clubs.

Search out these teams and find the ones that matter most to you. A few Etsy teams that I suggest you take a look at include the Epreneurship Team, the Handmadeology Team, and the Etsy Business Topic Team. You can explore Etsy Team by clicking on the word "community" in the top left-hand corner of the Etsy homepage and then on "teams."

Administration Tips, Tricks, and Nuggets

Here are some tips, tricks, and nuggets to help you run the administrative tasks that accompany your Etsy business.

23. Productivity Killers

Nothing kills your business like wasting time. The biggest time wasters, which may masquerade as work for Etsy sellers, is surfing on Etsy, hanging out in the forums too long, reading too many blogs, and hanging out on social media sites with no purpose in mind. The solution to productivity loss is time management. Set time limits, so you can spend less time on, or completely avoid, the activities that may waste your time.

24. Choosing a Camera

Every year, new cameras come out with improved features. And since good product photography is one of the top components for making sales on Etsy, every Etsy seller needs a good camera. When my wife started selling on Etsy, we found out right away that purchasing a new camera for her business was a top priority. While it can be a costly purchase for a business that is starting out, I consider it a necessity. Some of the most important features you should look for include a macro setting (which gives you the ability to take close-up photos), 8 or 10-plus megapixels to take crisp large photos, and a manual mode that allows you to adjust the ISO and white balance. On the Chapter 9 web page of Etsy-preneurship.com, I have included an analysis of some of the most popular cameras used by Etsy sellers, along with an explanation of these cameras' respective strengths and weaknesses. There is a camera in every Etsy seller's price range that can do a good job. The formula for taking good product photos is a good camera plus good technique plus practice. Having a good camera is the first part to mastering good product photos.

25. Product Photography Technique

The second part of having good product photos is good technique. I never had to learn product photography techniques, because I was typically taking photos of e-books or spreadsheets. With that said, I'll leave this topic to the photography experts in the blog articles I've included in the downloadable "Must-Read Etsy List (Top 100)" of articles. I can tell you that my wife used a homemade lightbox, had powerful lights, and read and practiced her technique until she got it right!

26. Packaging

All Etsy sellers must decide how their products will be packaged. Some Etsy sellers opt for no packaging, while others choose packaging that is quite impressive and creative. The best way to decide on your Etsy shop's packaging is to look at what competitors are doing and read about packaging tips from multiple Etsy sellers to find what is right for your business. Some customers value packaging, while others don't care about it at all. Remember to consider the cost and effort of packaging when pricing your products.

27. Customer Service

Good customer service makes average shops good and good shops great! Good customer service is hard to define but easy to recognize when you see it. My customer service philosophy involves treating others the way they want to be treated, answering all questions, and underpromising and overdelivering (i.e., exceeding customers' expectations). As a download for this chapter, you will also find an e-book interview with Lori Patton (of Heartworks by Lori) about customer service, which is something she does very well. It certainly shows in her shop and feedback.

28. To-Do Lists

Some people hate to-do lists, and others love them. In the end, you need to make sure you have a method to get things done in your Etsy shop in a timely manner—doing the important things and skipping the unimportant things. I like creating a daily to-do list on a little yellow sticky note, and as I perform the tasks I cross them off. I do this digitally, too, but it is much more fulfilling for me to cross out an item with a pen when a task is complete. I am constantly breaking down large goals into smaller tasks, thus giving me momentum.

29. Shipping

Different types of products and customer expectations require different shipping methods. In the supplemental reading list, I have included various Etsy sellers' tips, tricks, and nuggets so you can learn from them and make shipping a smooth process for your business.

30. Work/Life Balance

All Etsy sellers have to balance their other responsibilities and relationships with their business. Starting and running a small business is an emotional and financial experience requiring a huge time investment. Your decisions will impact the quality of life of other people. Long hours are often a calling card for some small business owners, but I do not believe it has to be that way. I like focused hard work for shorter periods of time versus relaxed work over ridiculously long hours. I once worked in the auditing profession, where working 60 to 80 hours per week is a badge of honor. It is appropriate to occasionally work hours like this, but life is not all work and no play. You are your own boss, so you can set the hours you want to abide by. For some people, work is often such fun that they don't even consider it work; even so, make sure you don't become a workaholic. Read the supplemental articles to learn how other Etsy sellers balance being a mom, dad, or spouse with being a full-time employee. You will see articles about how some sellers balance all the components of their work lives and personal lives.

Promotional Tips, Tricks, and Nuggets

Promotions and marketing are some of the steepest learning curves that new Etsy sellers must master. While Chapter 8 ("Marketing") gave you a framework and a discipline by which to operate your business, it did not tell you all the specific techniques. That would have required multiple books! Here are some areas of specific marketing techniques and methods that you can learn more about and implement for your business by reading the supplemental articles.

31. Google Analytics

Google Analytics is similar to Etsy Shop Statistics, except Google Analytics is much more in depth. I typically use Etsy shop stats, because they are easier to digest. However, I review my shop's Google Analytics page regularly to see other trends that Etsy does not track, like average time on the site by visitors, the bounce rate (how many visitors left your page from the page they entered), and how many new visitors there were. Setting up Google Analytics requires Etsy sellers to follow some specific steps. It is also a specific skill to be able to interpret Google Analytic reports. I have included articles on both setup and interpretation to help you become a Google Analytics expert. Before Etsy shop stats, all Etsy sellers who wanted data on their shop's traffic had to use Google Analytics.

32. Search Engine Optimization (SEO)

Search engine optimization is a concept that allows your products or web pages to increase in web searches (Google, Bing, Yahoo!, and Etsy searches). Here are some tips from Timothy Adam (of Handmadeology.com), one of the best experts in SEO for Etsy sellers:

> *Getting your Etsy Shop and Etsy items found on Google can be a difficult task, but with the proper research and placement of specific keywords, you can begin to dominate small niches and move up in the Google search. There are a few things you need to keep in mind when you are looking for keywords to use. When looking for keywords and phrases, the three most important factors that determine a good keyword are shopper intent, search volume, and keyword competition.*
>
> *1. Shopper intent. The most important factor to look at when figuring out the value of a keyword or phrase is intent. When picking a good keyword or phrase to analyze, pick words or phrases that people*

interested in your items would search for. You know your product best, so use words that you would use to search for your products.

2. Volume. *When determining the value of a keyword or phrase, you need to look at the search volume. Are there enough people searching per month for a term on Google to even consider optimizing for it?*

3. Keyword competition. *A keyword can have a high search volume on Google, but that does not mean it is a good keyword or phrase. You have to know how many competing pages there are according to Google and the competition on Etsy.*

33. Using Coupons on Etsy

Etsy allows sellers to offer their customers coupons or discount codes as an incentive to make purchases. The use of coupons can be a way to reward existing customers, to bring in new customers, and even to track how customers found your Etsy shop. You can create and manage your coupons by clicking on "your shop" in the top right-hand corner of Etsy's homepage and then clicking "coupon codes" on the left sidebar. Coupons create a buzz around your shop and give you an easy way to run promotions and sales and create hype around your business. Everyone loves a sale!

34. Selling Bundles, Packages, and Subscriptions

I have found that selling bundles, packages, and subscriptions are a natural way for Etsy sellers to increase the average selling price in their shop. If you make only products that sell for $4, you can bundle 10 of them together and sell them for $30. This gives the customer an incentive to make a larger purchase while giving your shop a higher price point. Etsy sellers can also put related items together for sale in packages. For example, if you sell gloves and jackets in your shop, why not offer a package that includes the gloves and jacket together?

Last, consider selling a subscription for your product. If you sell hair bows for baby girls, you could put together a group of 12 bows (one per month) that a customer can order and receive throughout the year. These three selling techniques are easy ways to give your customers value and savings by putting multiple products together, which also increases your sales volume and provides variety in your products.

35. Selling Gift Cards on Etsy

If you offer gift cards for purchase, customers who love your shop can give gift cards to those they think would also enjoy your shop. There are some creative ways and methods devised by Etsy sellers to start selling gift cards for their Etsy shops. I suggest you explore these by reading the related articles on this topic.

36. Black Friday, Cyber Monday, and Other Peak Selling Days

From around Thanksgiving until Christmas, most Etsy sellers can experience a major growth spurt in their business. This holiday rush starts near those holidays that are focused on shopping. On Black Friday, the day after Thanksgiving, shoppers start shopping aggressively for Christmas gifts. Cyber Monday, the first Monday after Thanksgiving, is when many online retailers offer sales. The holiday rush is trending to start earlier and earlier each year, and new holidays are being created all the time (e.g., "Sofa Saturday," for shopping via electronic tablets, and "Small Business Saturday," created by American Express). The bottom line here is that your Etsy shop needs a plan to capitalize on these increased sale days. If you do nothing, you might notice a small increase in sales, but if you have a well-thought-out and well-implemented plan, you could see your shop explode with sales during the holiday rush. Managing the holiday rush well can turn an average year into a blockbuster. The holiday rush provides a glimmer of hope during the slower times of the year when sales might not be where you would like them.

During the typical holiday rush, you are busy filling orders, shipping, and marketing your products, yet I believe there are other seasons that Etsy shops go through during the year: a "preparation-for-the-holiday-rush season," a "learning season," a "shop-cleanup season," a "coast-and-let-things-run season," a "season of change," a "season of experimentation," a "season of vacation," and a "season of long hours." I encourage you to ask yourself, every few weeks, which season your business is in. No season lasts forever, and being aware of your business's season gives you confidence in how you are operating your business and what you are focusing your time on.

The final four tips, tricks, and nuggets highlight some of the most popular social media sites. The content that could be included for these topics is enormous. There are individuals who have specialized knowledge in each of these fields, and I will rely on pointing you to their content through the downloadable article list. All of these sites and marketing methods take some time to learn, and I suggest you learn to do one of them well rather than attempt to do all four with mediocrity. Some Etsy sellers excel in all four of these disciplines, but more often than not, I see Etsy sellers focusing on a few of these methods with excellence.

37. Blogging Tips

Here are some of the most common topics of Etsy sellers' blogs: their products, new product lines, their personal lives, stories about their business, promotions, sales, and coupons, learning a new product technique, insight into the day-to-day operations of their business, new skills they learn, new materials they are using, features about other Etsy sellers, interviews with other Etsy sellers they admire, reviews of other products, schedules of events or giveaways, and sharing how-tos.

If you would talk to your friend about it, you can share it on a blog. Make sure you keep your blog updated, and don't go for long periods of time without providing new content, as your readers will then eventually fall away. Remember to track your trends with Google Analytics for your blog. You will need to also make sure that you purchase your domain name (yourbusinessname.com). I have included links to popular domain registration services on the Chapter 9 web page of Etsy-preneurship.com.

38. Facebook Tips

Facebook allows more interaction between you and your customers/fans. You can respond easily to their messages, ask them questions, and see their feedback through likes and shares they provide to you. An Internet *meme* refers to a concept that spreads throughout the Internet rapidly. Memes are typically funny or amusing and encourage people to share them with others; they often spread rapidly from person to person (called *virality*). Viral marketing can rapidly increase the exposure of your business to new customers. I have two fun examples of business-related memes designed for marketing purposes:

Etsy sellers' meme. One afternoon I took about an hour to create a funny picture about Etsy sellers; I posted it on Facebook. It was immediately liked 262 times and shared 165 times. These 165 shares put the picture on their respective Facebook walls for all their friends and fans to see. From all these shares, eventually close to 2,000 new Facebook fans were gained. It was also viewed 5,000 times on a blog and pinned more than 200 times on Pinterest. Not bad for an hour's work! If you want to view this meme, you should become a fan of Etsy-preneurship on Facebook and search my pictures! Feel free to like and share this to continue its exposure to others.

Football joke video. I am a Broncos football fan and got caught up in the hype about Tim Tebow during the 2011 season. I created a short video joke that was 90 seconds long. It took about three hours to put together, but it was really fun to do. I posted it on YouTube and shared it on Facebook, and within a month, it had about 24,000 views. Tim Tebow doesn't even play for the Broncos anymore! You can find this video by searching "Tim Tebow & Tom Brady Joke" on YouTube.

These two examples show the power of thinking outside the box when it comes to marketing your business. Following the everyday rules gets you only so far. I haven't shared my meme ideas that flopped! Creating something that is viral takes a little bit of good timing and the right content and delivery.

39. Twitter Tips

Using Twitter requires you to know Twitter-speak—hashtags (#), @signs, following, tweeters, tweets, replies, direct message, retweets, and shortened URLs. When sharing these short, 144-character messages, be yourself and share your products and your news, retweet others, comment with others, and share links and information that are useful to your followers. Twitter is like a conversation with your customers and fans.

40. Pinterest Tips

Using Pinterest for Etsy sellers is still a developing marketing technique, but good photos continue to rule the day. Check out the related articles to find some cutting-edge ideas on how Etsy sellers can maximize their Etsy shop's exposure on Pinterest.

Download: Sales Countdown Goal Tracker, Customer Service E-Book, and Must-Read Etsy Articles (Top 100) List

Note: To download this document, please go to www.etsy-preneurship.com/downloads.

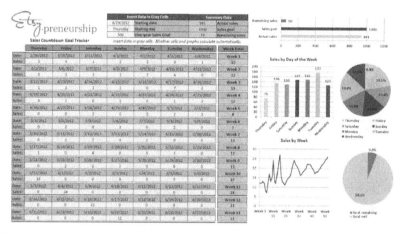

There are three downloads for Chapter 9. The first is the "Sales Countdown Goal Tracker," which allows you to set sales goals for your Etsy shop and track these for an entire year.

Note: To download this document, please go to www.etsy-preneurship.com/downloads.

Customer Service E-book: Interview with Lori Patton of Heartworks By Lori

The second download is a great interview with Lori Patton, of Heartworks by Lori, covering all the

important topics about the role of customer service in an Etsy shop.

Note: To download this document, please go to www.etsy-preneurship.com/downloads.

13. Etsy Shop Categories
Etsy: Seller How-to: Guiding Buyers with Shop Sections http://www.etsy.com/blog/en/2008/seller-how-to-guiding-buyers-with-shop-sections/
MeaganVisser: Revamping Your Etsy Shop – Shop Sections, Rearranging Your Shop, & Featured Listings With Kimberly of Cinnamon Spice http://www.meaganvisser.com/2011/03/revamping-your-etsy-shop-2011-shop-sections-rearranging-your-shop-and-featured-listings-with-kimberly-of-cinnamon-spice/
14. Etsy Product Descriptions
Handmadeology: Writing Expert Product Descriptions for Your Etsy Shop http://www.handmadeology.com/writing-expert-product-descriptions-for-your-etsy-shop/
Handmade Success: 5 Step Formula for Writing Handmade Product Descriptions that Sell http://handmadesuccess.com/2011/04/5-step-formula-for-writing-handmade-product-descriptions-that-sell/
15. Renewing Product on Etsy
Etsytips: Renew..Re-List... Rinse . . . Repeat . . . Really http://etsytips.com/re-list-re-list-rinse-repeat/
Handmadeology: A Few Alternatives To Renewing Etsy Items http://www.handmadeology.com/a-few-alternaives-to-renewing-etsy-items/
16. Etsy Search Ads
Etsy: Lear About Search Ads on Etsy http://www.etsy.com/search-ads/
Handmadeology: Etsy Serach Ad Strategem Helping Etsy Sellers Become "Ad Smart" http://www.handmadeology.com/etsy-search-ad-stratagem-helping-etsy-sellers-become-ad-smart/
17. Etsy Conversations (Convos)
Etsy: Conversations http://www.etsy.com/help/article/483#conversations
18. Etsy Relevancy Search
Handmadeology: The Etsy Relevancy Free Report and Checklist http://www.handmadeology.com/the-etsy-relevancy-breakdown-free-report-and-checklist/
Etsy: Putting Your Shop on top Etsy's Most Relevant Search http://www.etsy.com/blog/en/2011/putting-your-shop-on-top-etsy%E2%80%99s-most-relevant-search/
19. Etsy Circles
Etsy: What is my Circle? http://www.etsy.com/help/article/354
Designing an MBA: Using Etsy's Circles and Activity Feeds to Research Your Ideal Customer http://designinganmba.com/2010/12/16/etsy-circles-market-research/
20. Etsy Seller Handbook
Etsy: Etsy Seller Handbook http://www.etsy.com/blog/en/category/seller-handbook/ (Note: A must read! This is Etsy's blog for sellers.)
21. Etsy Feedback

The third download is a list of must-read articles that correspond to the 40 tips, tricks, and nuggets covered in this chapter.

Chapter 10

Practicing Business Self-Development

So far, we've started a strong business foundation with a business plan and learned about the six core business foundations (bookkeeping, taxes, finances, legal, operations, and marketing). Then we built on that foundation by receiving tips, tricks, and nuggets from sellers in the Etsy community. Now it is time to develop that foundation. Developing your business foundation is largely all about self-development. Businesses are always changing, and when a business owner becomes stale, the business eventually becomes stale, too. Developing your business foundation is a process that never stops, as you learn and become an expert in more and more business-related topics. Small business owners wear many different hats, and this requires an owner to be a lifelong learner.

Developing the Foundation

Most Etsy sellers are sole proprietors, and although it is very exciting to set your own hours, call all the shots, and choose the path for your business, it can also be lonely sometimes. This chapter is all about the support group behind your business. While you are the driving force behind your business, many individuals behind the scenes can help you succeed. I have reviewed and included nine of the best websites to help Etsy sellers run their Etsy businesses; I have also included seven Etsy applications (apps) to make your operations go more smoothly. Consider these 16 resources as your advisors, consultants, trusted counsel, and support team.

Self-development should be intentional. If you are not intentional about it, you are more than likely going to ignore it or forget about doing it. Self-development means reading about new business techniques, hearing new ideas in marketing and operational topics, and communicating with others who face similar business challenges. I typically think of self-development in two major phases:

1. Snack-size self-development. I try to learn new things every single day, and this type of self-development does not take a long time. Here are some easy ways to get more snack-size self-development opportunities in your life: Scan a handful of business-related blogs daily; subscribe to e-mail lists; follow your favorite small business resources on social media; read a chapter out of a book each day; read an article that catches your attention; and scan news headlines for important topics. Look for 5 to 10 opportunities to develop each day, and make it a part of your daily routine. I do this so frequently that I hardly even notice I am doing it. This type of self-development ensures you are always learning and never stagnant, but a diet of all snacks will not allow you to grow fully in the knowledge you need to make significant jumps in your business.

2. *Full-meal self-development.* These full-course self-development meals take time to complete and are more in-depth than the snack portions of self-development. Some ways that I get full-course self-development meals include reading books on business topics I know nothing about, finding e-courses or e-books on developing topics, attending seminars, viewing webinars, signing up for classes, seeking out one-on-one consultations with small business experts, and watching training videos. I try to do something more in-depth at least weekly or monthly (depending on my schedule). These full-course self-development meals are where your business can really grow in leaps and bounds. It takes time to master a new business technique, and you can't learn everything you need to know in just a five-minute time block. I can look back at some books that I have read that have changed the way I think, conferences that have helped shaped my values and vision, and training that has given me the confidence to try new things. This type of self-development is a business game changer!

The resources in this chapter will give you the snack-size and full-meal self-development you need. I am friends with some of these resource and app developers; I communicate regularly with many of them; and I am very aware of the content, services, and skills they all have. The Etsy support community is alive and well! Enjoy exploring these resources and practicing your continual self-development!

The Top Etsy Seller Resources

Here is a list (in no particular order) of the best small-business-related resources for Etsy sellers to visit to make their small business better. For each site, I have included a little about the site's content, its owner/editor, and a few comments about the site.

Handmadeology

Handmadeology.com exists for the purpose of teaching artists how to successfully sell their handmade goods online and to feature the newest handmade, vintage, and supply items found on Etsy. Handmadeology offers new content daily to help Etsy sellers run their businesses. Typical topics include social media how-tos, Etsy tips, Etsy news, and many free downloadable tools and e-courses. The downloads include Etsy Sales Goal Tracker, Handmade Twitter Blueprint, Etsy Relevancy Breakdown and Checklist, Social Media Blitz E-course, Your Business Identity E-course, and Etsy Traffic Log Goal Tracker. Handmadeology also offers additional content (videos, spreadsheets, and e-books) to all "Handmadeology PRO" members, a monthly members-only version of the site.

The site is run by editor Timothy Adam and his Handmadeology team. He is a self-taught metal artist and a certified MIG welder. He started designing modern metal furniture in 2004 and built his first piece in Baltimore with his sister-in-law, who is a furniture designer. Tim found his passion in metal and kept on designing and building. He struggled for four years to make a name in local galleries in the Grand Rapids, Michigan, area. His friend introduced him to Etsy in February of 2007, and it changed his business. He started creating a jewelry line and has not turned back. In November of 2007, Tim quit his full-time job, because his passion was becoming a dream come true! He now sells his products all over the world through his Etsy shop, and his wholesale accounts around the country include galleries, museums, and salons.

Notes from Jason: I highly recommend Handmadeology. Be sure to check out the free downloads. Make sure to sign up for the e-mail list to be notified of important Etsy business topics. Check out Handmadeology Pro, a monthly membership site in which I am also a contributing editor.

Heartmade

Mayi Carles is the energetic and entertaining editor of Heartmadeblog.com. In fact, she sent an e-mail to me in her very own words:

I love party props + my Eeyore pj's + cupcakes . . . oh my! If left unsupervised, I could eat an entire batch of Red Velvets. And here goes, the self-proclaimed job title (drum roll please): I'm an artistic inventor + organizational master + pocket-size creative business fairy—just a fancy way of saying that my 10 little fingers have a severe creative addiction + that I beat mess for a living + that my T-rex-size heart has a monstrous appetite to empower others to break down their barriers to success + turn their passions into profit + make a real difference in the world. I believe that throughout our life there's a voice that only you can hear—it's a call to why you're here. Hearing it + heeding it is the greatest gift you can ever give yourself + to the world. I also know that if you silence it, something magical will be lost, something unique + beautiful that only you can give. So, if you're ready to let go of who you think you should be to dream bigger + imagine better + achieve more + embrace all the beautiful messiness in between, come join me at Heartmade Blog. At Heartmade we're starting a revolution against safety blankets + the lure of perfectionism + inside-the-box paradigms to make room for your splendidly epic life in progress + that pounding passionate heart of yours, too. So come on over! Yes you, in your paint-stained pajamas if you wish. This is your space to spill open your gifts + hopes + fears + epiphanies + worries + questions + more. You're bound to leave here feeling lighter + empowered + most certainly loved.

Notes from Jason: This is a great place to go if you learn well by video and is one of the most entertaining Etsy resources available.

Etsy-preneurship

Etsy-preneurship.com is where you are going to receive each chapter's download, but it is also a place where I keep you updated with Etsy news, editorials, and analysis. Sign up for the e-mail list to stay notified of important topics about practicing the art of Etsy-preneurship. If you enjoy this book and its downloads, you will love Etsy-preneurship!

Notes from Jason: Remember to also follow me on Facebook, Twitter, and Pinterest! I love Etsy-preneurship.com!

Meagan Visser

MeaganVisser.com exists for the purpose of teaching moms how to successfully start and grow a creative business around their families. The focus is on simplifying basic business principles, marketing, time management, and the infamous work/life balance. MeaganVisser.com offers content to help moms push past their fears and struggles to build the business of their dreams. Typical topics include branding, blogging, increasing traffic and sales, product development, productivity, social media, and more.

Formats range from written posts to screencast tutorials, videos, and podcasts. A variety of free and paid products and services are offered for business owners, plus a weekly newsletter, topical reports, digital guides, e-courses, and individual coaching.

The site is run by Meagan Visser, a wife, mother, and serial entrepreneur. Her love for helping other moms make their creative passions come to life and become more profitable is her primary goal in business. She has always looked for ways to make money from her many creative interests and, as a stay-at-home mom, has had many opportunities to pursue them to different degrees. Now, as a coach to other moms, she shares her struggles, triumphs, lessons learned, and the many new things she's constantly learning while living her many passions vicariously through her clients.

Notes from Jason: Meagan finds and creates some of the best content for Etsy sellers to digest easily. She offers great ideas from a mom's perspective.

ArtBusiness

ArtBusiness.com provides complete art consulting and advisory services, art appraisals, art price data, articles for artists and collectors, and market research and information to anyone involved with art. Services include appraising all works of fine art; consulting on buying, selling, donating, collecting, or otherwise transferring works of fine art; assistance with inheritance issues involving art; research, documentation, organization, and assistance in settlement or dissemination of artist estates; assistance in resolving disputes or disagreements over art; and expert testimony and opinions in legal cases involving art.

Consulting is available for artists at all stages in their careers on matters including organizing and presenting their art, writing about their art, getting assistance with situations involving formal agreements or representation of their art, marketing, promotion, pricing individual or multiple works of art, approaching the marketplace, targeting specific venues for possible shows or sales, website functionality, selling online, self-representation, exhibiting and selling at galleries or alternative venues, long-term career development, estate issues, and appraisal and documentation of individual pieces or larger bodies of work.

ArtBusiness.com contains more than 3,000 pages of free content, more than 50,000 images, regularly posted art business articles, art gallery reviews and openings, art critiques, art market news, critical evaluations of specialized technical art reference books, CD-ROMs, and online databases. Out-of-print and rare art reference books and exhibition catalogs are also available through the site.

Notes from Jason: The content here is detailed, thorough, and presented in a very professional manner. I am most impressed with the high quality of content that is provided.

Papernstitch

Papernstitch.com opened its virtual doors in 2008 to showcase the work of talented artists and artisans while promoting a creative, handmade lifestyle. The brand is broken down into two main parts, an exhibition site and a blog, which both serve as positive outlets for creative sellers from around the world to come together, find support, and be found. There are hundreds of thousands of sellers on Etsy, so the exhibition site helps narrow the search when you looking for quality handmade items to purchase. The Papernstitch blog is updated twice daily and is a mixture of original do-it-yourself projects, handmade features, and small business articles, podcasts, and videos for creative entrepreneurs. This blog focuses on running a successful online shop, getting noticed by popular bloggers and magazine editors, tackling social media on your own, and more.

Brittni Mehlhoff, the founder and editor at Papernstitch, has been surrounded by creative women since she was a child, sitting by her grandmother's sewing machine and watching her work on her newest quilt design. After receiving a BFA in painting and drawing, Brittni started two different galleries with a group of fellow artists and a digital magazine featuring artists and designers in her city, all while pursuing her own work as a painter and participating in exhibitions regionally and around the country. While working as a high school art teacher, she joined the online game and opened a shop, along with a few buddies, and quickly realized it was going to be a struggle to get her work seen in the sea of handmade art on the Internet. She figured if she was having this problem, others must be experiencing similar issues, which ultimately led her to create Papernstitch.

Notes from Jason: I really like how Papernstitch is a great place to be inspired by new products and new business ideas. If you ever feel as though you are in a business or creativity rut, this is the place to go.

Create as Folk

Createasfolk.com is an oasis for creative types longing to thrive at meaningful work. Resources are designed specifically for creative entrepreneurs who want to discover their unique value and communicate that in a fun and profitable way. Think clarity + service + style = cash. The blog offers short videos and focuses on providing inspiration and actionable information for creative solo entrepreneurs in areas such as time management, money wrangling, business planning, blogging with purpose, and behind-the-scenes peeks into how Create as Folk is run. The pay-what-it's-worth-to-you e-guide "Roadmap to Action" is available for those who want to stop chasing their tail and instead master their own way of working. One-on-one coaching addresses everything from the very foundations of your business (e.g., who you are, who you serve, and why you do it) to developing services to creating a website worth talking about.

Notes from Jason: Create as Folk offers some neat downloads (e.g., free blog planner) and is a great place to learn how your actions can come into alignment with your ideal life and business.

Scoutie Girl

Scoutiegirl.com is a daily zine, or online magazine, with the aim of getting you thinking about your creative life and the changing world around you. This site allows you to connect, converse, and commune with other extraordinarily creative women and men. Get inspired. Get informed.

According to Scoutie Girl:

Scoutie Girl is written by a passionate staff of thinkers, makers, and designers who share a unique vision for our 21st century bespoke culture. We see the New Economy—one led by visionaries, creatives, and right-brained thinkers—as viewed through a "handmade" lens. The rise of indie craft, Etsy, and DIY proves that innovation is alive and well in our world. And we know that you're looking for more than pretty pictures to quench your thirst for new paradigm living. Explore your world by answering big questions, connecting with diverse people, and finding common ground with a worldwide community. You are Scoutie Girl—and so are we. Scoutie Girl is run by two brilliant women. Tara Gentile is a thought leader in the DIY culture and creativity sphere. She's a respected business coach, blogger, and motivator who empowers passionate people to build a business around what they love while laughing their way to the bank. Carrie Keplinger is the chief post wrangler, advertising manager, and communications specialist who also works with microbusiness owners on public relations and online marketing.

Notes from Jason: Scoutie Girl is the place to go if you want to see where the handmade scene is going in the near future—innovation, passion, and vision are present here.

Smaller Box

Smallerbox.net is a go-to resource for the creative businessperson. Founder and writer Meredith Keller gives advice based on firsthand experience in starting and growing a successful product-based business. The site includes an information-rich blog and a resource guide that lists both premium and free tools that creative entrepreneurs need to grow a business. Smaller Box also provides advertising opportunities for independent designers via co-op advertising website called I Shop Indie. Smaller Box delves into topics such as publicity, branding, viral marketing, social media, e-mail marketing, and conversion rate optimization. Regular readers at Smaller Box appreciate Meredith's pull-no-punches writing style and ability to make technical and advanced topics accessible.

Meredith brings the expertise she's derived from running Ex-Boyfriend, a clothing and accessory company started in 2009. Ex-Boyfriend has shipped products to every inhabited continent on the planet and has had products featured on popular network TV shows, on blogs, and in magazines.

Notes from Jason: The thing I like best about Smaller Box is how practical the content is. Right after reading or watching the content, I feel I can go out and implement it right away.

A Few Other Sites

I suggest you also check out DesignSponge.com, DesigninganMBA.com, OhMyHandmade.com, Craftbuds.com, and Meylah.com/meylah for additional small business resources that are popular with many Etsy sellers.

Top Etsy Seller Apps

Etsy has released its API code, which allows developers to build their own apps for the web, desktop, and mobile devices. Following are the apps for sellers that I believe offer some of the best services for Etsy sellers. I have included links to all these apps on Etsy-preneurship.com for your reference. Additional useful apps can be found at www.etsy.com/apps/.

Promotesy

This tool makes promoting and implementing your 30-day marketing plan really easy. It allows you to manage your social media promotions on multiple social networks at the same time. With a few clicks, you can automate your marketing plan for days, weeks, and months ahead. This helps you provide structure and discipline to your 30-day marketing plan. The social networks currently covered by Promotesy include Facebook, Twitter, LinkedIn, and Pinterest. Promotesy does have a small monthly fee, but can easily more than pay for itself in the amount of time it saves you.

Etsy On Sale

Etsyonsale.com won Etsy's 2010 Handmade Code API Contest and provides three main services to Etsy sellers. First, the Sales Event Manager allows you to put all or some of your shop items on sale and schedule when the sales take place (immediately or in the future). Second, the Auto Renew feature allows you to schedule when you want your Etsy listings to renew automatically. Third, its Tag Tool allows you to edit all or part of your listing's tags easily. Sellers do have to pay to receive credits to perform these activities.

FotoFuze

Fotofuze.com gives you the tools to make your product photos look more professional by removing the background and leaving only the product. This allows you to have the famous white-background-only photos that are very popular on Etsy. The app allows you to create, update, renew, copy, and draft listings while in Fotofuze.com. This service is free for Etsy sellers.

Craftopolis

Craftopolis.com offers three tools that can help Etsy sellers run their business. First, Shop Lovers allows sellers to view sales, hearts, views, and Google Analytics data in a calendar view. Second, the Edit Express feature is a batch-editing tool to change prices, titles, descriptions, and item quantities. Third, Tag Report gives sellers a way to view the search terms that individuals are using to find your shop and product, thus giving you data to determine which keywords are working the best for you. These services are free.

Etsy for iPhone

Etsy for iPhone is the Etsy you know and love for the iPhone or iPod. Buyers can shop and purchase handmade and vintage items and view Treasury lists. Sellers can access listings and orders and operate their business on the go. This app is free.

BETSI: Bulk/Batch Editing Tool

BETSI is a bulk/batch editing application that gives you information about your listings that you are working so you can make the appropriate changes. BETSI Live Listing Titles update in real time, allowing you to feel confident that the changes you have implemented are really working live. There is a free trial for Etsy sellers to see how BETSI works.

Treasury Shop and Treasury Widget

If you love Etsy treasuries, you will enjoy this tool. Treasury Shop allows you to browse treasuries at a glance through a 3D wall view. You can view these by the top 300 most popular treasuries, the top 300 treasuries with the most comments, and the top 300 newly listed treasuries. You can also search treasuries by tags, title, or curator. This app is free.

Download: Self-Development Resource Guide and Learning Opportunity Planner

Note: To download this document, please go to www.etsy-preneurship.com/downloads.

Visit the sites that we covered in this chapter and then develop your specific learning plan. Remember to include both snack-size opportunities and full-course meal opportunities in your plan.

Chapter 11

Encouragement and Next Steps

We have built a firm foundation regarding business plans, bookkeeping, taxes, finances, legal topics, operations, and marketing. We have explored tips from the Etsy community, including how to develop yourself using other small business resources. What happens next? You are about to start planning your next steps, but I think there is one more thing you need before your Etsy business takes on the world—*encouragement.*

Encouragement energizes and powers success by strengthening hope, passion, and purpose. I think one of the best ways to be encouraged is to hear firsthand testimony from other Etsy sellers about their journey selling on Etsy. I have interviewed four Etsy sellers, all of whom I consider to be success stories. All are at different points in their small business journeys, and they have a variety of skills, passions, and profit levels. Even though these Etsy sellers have great Etsy businesses, I have not asked them for specific business-related tips, but have tried to learn more about the heart, the why, and the hopes that make up their respective Etsy businesses. I believe you will find that their hopes, dreams, and stories are not too different from yours—or from what you desire your Etsy story to become. Every Etsy success story is different, and these people are not superheroes—they are just like you, putting their hopes and dreams on the line as one small part of the greater Etsy community. I have included brief excerpts from their interviews in this book. The full interviews can be found as a downloadable e-book in Chapter 11 of Etsy-preneurship.com. Be encouraged as you learn and hear from these great Etsy shop owners who have gone before you and are also part of your Etsy community!

Real-Life Etsy-preneurs

An Etsy-preneur is an individual who practices Etsy-preneurship. Take heart as you hear the stories of these four Etsy-preneurs.

Heartworks by Lori

I have been selling photo and art lockets on Etsy since December 2007. My wearable works of art exude passion for artistic imagery, which translates into timeless designs and wearable dreams. My pieces have found their way into museums, hotels, and stores across the globe, as well as into the hearts and homes of loyal collectors worldwide.

Q In what ways has Etsy improved your personal finances?

A It's been a huge blessing to be able to sell my jewelry on Etsy and make a profit from it. Over the years, I've used some of my Etsy income to add to a large down payment to buy our very first home! That just thrills me, knowing that from the work of my hands I was able to contribute thousands of dollars to purchase a new house. As I continued to expand my business, I was able to purchase the truck that my wonderful and supportive husband has been eyeing for years! I love to be generous, and there's nothing better than surprising your spouse with his favorite vehicle on Christmas. All compliments of selling on Etsy! My next financial goal is to put aside money for my boy's college tuition. I'm determined to work hard at my business to help plan for their futures. I'm overjoyed that I can play a part in contributing to that.

Q What has been the most rewarding aspect of running a business on Etsy?

A I love to bring a smile to the face of my customers! The handmade locket that they just bought is made by two real hands with a heart behind it, and it brings me as the seller and the buyer into a more community-felt environment, which makes the big, huge world just a little smaller and down-home. I try to make the web-based buying process more friendly and personal, which makes it seem more like they're buying from a trusted friend rather than a sterile big-box company. I treat each buyer as an important person who deserves my personal communication, and that's how great business relationships are built. For me, creating photo and art lockets goes beyond just the surface level of wanting to create unique jewelry with art and photos. For me, these tiny treasures are keys of inspiration and meaning that fuel my fire and ignite my passion for what I do and why I sell on Etsy.

Note from Jason: Make sure to read Lori's interview on customer service from the Chapter 9 download.

RetroChalet

I have a background in marketing, which by day I use in my "real job" as the marketing representative for my husband, who is a famous barbecue guy. My Etsy shop stems from the things I love and collect, which are vintage! I sell vintage and handmade items: Melmac dinnerware from the 1950s, porcelain glove molds, industrial relics, kitschy stuff, and some of my handmade assemblage art. I started selling when I really stocked up the store in 2009, but have been dabbling on Etsy since 2007. My real name is Cindy Fahnestock-Schafer, but I write professionally under the name of Ira Mency. I run a blog on retro Melmac dinnerware history and try to persuade others to collect and love vintage items in the hope of keeping these items out of the landfill—and needing fewer mass-produced items. I do very well on Etsy, but I work at this only part-time, thanks to my real job, which has travel demands (thus making it difficult to do this full-time).

Q How has Etsy changed your life for the better?

A When I first opened my second shop (now closed) and started selling my assemblage art, I was immediately picked up and asked to include it in a museum event in North Carolina. It was very exciting, since I never had my art out there before. Soon, I was able to use this artwork to raise thousands of dollars for charity events. It if weren't for Etsy, this would not have happened to me, and I wouldn't have been able to achieve my hopes and dreams to raise money for my favorite charities. I have Etsy to thank for that. Etsy has allowed me to meet some of the kindest people I have ever met. I did a private fund-raiser for a farmer in Ames, Iowa, who was homeless (his house burned down and he had no insurance); I didn't even know him. I heard about his story from an Etsy seller. Before I knew it, tons of Etsy sellers were sending money in envelopes to this farmer and donating money to someone none of us knew. We raised over $1,400, and it was a legit cause!

Q What personal development have you seen in yourself since selling on Etsy?

A I know this sounds corny, but Etsy has given me the power to create a style—my style! Not only did it help get my artwork noticed, but it allows me to offer the items I like and others are now embracing. You can create your own style and share with others, and that really makes you feel good.

Jen's Closet

I have three shops: Jen's Closet was the first one I started in 2008; My Milk Glass Shop was started about a year after that; and The China Girl is my latest venture! Jen's Closet is full of an eclectic mix of vintage items—from fine china to Pyrex and cute, kitschy items. My name is Jennifer Beaton, but most people know me as Jen. What I am most proud of is being a mom (daughter Katherine, son Mark, and daughter Lindsey). Lindsey was the one who encouraged me to start my Etsy shop after I was laid off from my job in 2008 (a perfect part-time job I had for many years). Starting my Etsy shop was the best thing I could ever do, besides having my wonderful children! I love all aspects of running a shop. I had been pursuing a marketing degree, so this fulfills my passion for marketing through Twitter, Facebook, and Pinterest. Customer service is important to me as a consumer, so I want to give the absolute best customer service I can.

Q How has Etsy changed your life for the better?

A First, it has made me realize that if you work hard at something you love, you can make a living at it. I meet new people every day, some while shopping for items for my shop, some as new customers, and some through my favorite social media site, Twitter. I have a ton of followers there (jenscloset is my Twitter name).

Q What was your most encouraging sale or interaction with a customer?

A I've had so many! I love seeing the nice comments left on my feedback. What I really love is when I receive a note from customers telling me how much they love their purchase—that makes my day! For them to take the time to let me know is so nice.

Q What does Etsy mean to you?

A The world! Maybe that's exaggerating a bit, but Etsy has changed my life for the better. I love running my Etsy shops. Etsy means a great, creative community.

JustJaynes

I have two Etsy shops, LydiaLayne and JustJaynes, selling hand-stamped and personalized jewelry. I started LydiaLayne in 2006 and JustJaynes in 2007. My name is Cathy, and I live in my hometown of Greenville, Michigan, with my husband, our dog Chuck, and our cat CC. After hibernating all winter, we spend our summers golfing, fishing, and camping. My business has gone through many changes. I started out making beaded necklaces. Today, you won't find a single beaded necklace in my shop! I had much success selling sterling silver charms as supplies. Then I started putting them on chains, alone or in clusters. I still wanted to do more creatively, so I learned to stamp on metal. I love making one-of-a-kind treasures for my customers.

Q How has Etsy changed your life for the better?

A Thanks to selling on Etsy, my dream of working from home full-time came true! After losing my job at the end of 2009, I started working full-time with JustJaynes in 2010.

Q What encouraging words do you have for Etsy sellers who are just starting out or looking to grow their business?

A Learn as much as you can about product photography, marketing, and promotion. While Etsy is a great venue for artists and crafters, don't let it be the only place you show your wares. Set up your own website! Use the free tools that are out there, such as Blogger, WordPress, Facebook, Twitter, and Pinterest. Also, be open to change, and always be looking for the next evolution of your product.

Practicing Etsy-preneurship and Finding Your Inner Etsy-preneur

This book is all about the how-to of running a business (i.e., teaching you the art and the science of Etsy-preneurship). Etsy-preneurship is made up of the core business foundations you need to know to succeed. Knowledge and tools give you confidence and empower you to succeed, but don't forget that you have another secret weapon to help you reach success . . . *you*!

The moment you start practicing Etsy-preneurship, you become an Etsy-preneur. All Etsy-preneurs have a unique set of personalities, dreams, skills, strengths, creativity, encouragement styles, and other individual attributes that can help you create a thriving business on Etsy. My encouragement to you is that, as you practice Etsy-preneurship, begin the process of finding the Etsy-preneur in you!

Your Internal Source of Encouragement

I hope the interviews from successful Etsy sellers have encouraged and inspired you. All encouragement comes from a source—either external or internal. The testimonies you have read are an external source of encouragement, although the Etsy sellers might have revealed their own internal encouragement sources. Other external sources of encouragement might include inspiring music, movies, or quotes. This type of encouragement is often short-lived. Long-lasting and deep reservoirs of encouragement come from inside of you. I believe that to run a successful business for the long haul, you need a deep spring of internal encouragement. I see this internal encouragement impacting your work, labor, and endurance. Work is produced by an encouragement source. Labor is prompted by an encouragement source. Endurance is inspired by an encouragement source. Let's explore these actions (work, labor, and endurance) separately:

- *Work produced by* ____. Work consists of the crafting and business skills you possess and how you use them in action.

Work is the finished inventory you create, the marketing campaign you run, and the operational disciplines you use in your day-to-day work. This work must be produced by an encouragement source. "Work produced by faith" is my personal encouragement source. My beliefs drive the products and quality of work I produce. How would you finish this phrase? "Work produced by ____." Other encouragement sources might include family, friends, passion, or experience.

- *Labor prompted by ____.* Labor is the time you put into your business when you could be taking a nap or resting. Labor is the drive to wake up in the morning and get started on making your business better. Labor is also the cost in financial resources you sacrifice to make your business succeed. This labor must be prompted by an encouragement source. "Labor prompted by love" is my personal encouragement source. My love for others (especially my family) encourages me to sacrifice time to provide all they need through my labor. How would you fill in this phrase? "Labor prompted by

____." Other encouragement sources might include perseverance, values, excellence, recognition, or subsistence.

- *Endurance inspired by* ____. Endurance is perseverance to continue when all you want to do is stop. Endurance is giving it one more try when it seems like nothing else is working. Endurance is carrying two heavy loads when the bare minimum was carrying one. This endurance must be inspired by an encouragement source. "Endurance inspired by hope" is my personal encouragement source. My hope in a better tomorrow from hard work today allows me to get through trying times. How would you complete this phrase? "Endurance inspired by ____." Other encouragement sources might include mission, purpose, calling, or determination.

Starting and running your own business comes with many challenges, but overcoming those challenges is very rewarding. Hold on to your internal encouragement sources tightly and let them produce work, prompt labor, and inspire endurance in your business.

What Do I Do Next?

This is it! You are about to really put the pedal down and start running your Etsy shop like the thriving business you want it to be. You can be encouraged that, if you have gone through this book, filled out the downloadable tools, and read the supplemental e-books and articles, you have a great foundation to build upon. You have a benefit over other Etsy sellers who have not built such a firm foundation. I have shared what you need to get started in creating a thriving business, and now it is time to take action and make it happen.

Planning, thinking, and daydreaming does not make a good business—action is the necessary catalyst that will turn your skills of Etsy-preneurship into the business you want to have. If you never try, you will never know how it turns out. The worst thing that can happen is that you fail, and that really isn't that big of a deal! Failure happens all the time, and failure often is the prerequisite to success. Action allows you to make progress and put your knowledge, strategies, and skills to the test. Don't take these next steps halfheartedly. Do the best you can and work hard. If you do this, you should have no regrets—you did your best!

What does doing your best and working hard look like to you? Let's better define this so you know what your next steps will look like.

- How many days do you think it will take you to confidently feel you can succeed on Etsy?
- How much time each day will you devote to reaching this success?
- What will you need to do during this time to become a success?

Starting and building a business takes a long time and more hours than you think. I wish I knew how many hours I have devoted to my small businesses, but I don't keep track! Don't sell yourself short by giving up too early or not giving yourself enough time to accomplish all the tasks you need to do.

I believe that the next 90 days will be very important for the success of your business. Three months is a sizable commitment, but also a reasonable amount of time for you to chase your dreams! Through the downloadable tool for this chapter, you will create a rough plan for the next 90 days and sign a commitment to work your hardest and do your very best. Work should always be done this way—any other way lacks passion and excellence.

I am cheering you on, just as I have cheered on many Etsy sellers before you. I want to hear from you about your success stories, about how you faced and overcame trouble and difficulty. Please send me a message and share your story with me and with others. Tell others of your Etsy-preneurship skills.

Please don't just read this book and not implement any of its suggestions without trying! Running a successful business on Etsy is fulfilling, and you will be a better person for doing it.

I wish you the best as you turn your Etsy-preneurship skills, knowledge, and tools into your own successful business on Etsy!

Download: Extended Interview E-Book and Next Steps— Commitment Statement and Planning Tool

I have provided the extended interviews from the beginning of this chapter if you are interested in learning more about these Etsy sellers' stories.

Note: To download this document, please go to www.etsy-preneurship.com/downloads.

Etsy-preneurship

Answer the questions. Sign and date. Share with others who will encourage you, hold you accountable for your goals, and support you in your efforts. Perform any additional detailed planning in your quest of success. You can do it! I know you can!

Next Steps—Commitment Statement and Planning Tool

Answer the following questions on your own paper or word processor to create your own personal commitment statement. Answer each question in one or two sentences.

What does the first level of success look like on Etsy for your business? (Don't think of the end goal 5 years from now, but a baby step you hope to make in the near future.)
"My first taste of success on Etsy will . . . "

How many days do you think it will take you to confidently feel you can reach this level of success?
"I will try to reach this level of success in _____ days."

How many hours a day will you devote to reaching this success?
"I will devote _____ hours a day to reach this goal."

What will you need to do during this time to become a success?
"I will _____, in my quest for success on Etsy."

What major projects will you need to work on?
"I will need to work on these special projects: _____."

What obstacles do you want to overcome?
"I will overcome these obstacles that face me: _____."

What support from others do you need during this time?
"I will receive the following support from the following people: _____."

What time of the day will you work?
"I will work during this time of the day: _____."

Defining your next step if you reach your goal:
"If I reach my baby step goal of success, my next step will be to _____."

Defining what you will do if you do not reach your goal:
"If I do not reach my goal, I will _____."

Day	Action Planned
Day 1	Write your day-by-day plan here.
Day 2	

Use this tool to write your own unique statement of commitment and to plan out your next 90 days. Now get going!

Advanced Application Internal Study

Etsy Shop Ratios

Your Etsy shop is full of stories, but you need to know where to look to find these stories. The stories are hidden in numbers that are found all over your Etsy shop. These stories can tell you interesting things about your business as well as predict the future performance of your Etsy shop. These stories are found in various ratios in your Etsy shop. A *ratio* is when you take two or more numbers and look at the relationship between them. Looking at these ratios is a type of business analysis, or analytics.

By looking at eight different data points in your Etsy shops, I can tell you seven stories (ratios) and provide three forecasts. The eight pieces of data are today's date, the date you opened your Etsy shop for business, the number of feedbacks you have received, the percentage of your feedback that is positive, the number of items you have for sale in your shop, how many items you have sold, how many shop hearts you have received, and the number of views of all the items in your shop. Let's go ahead and gather that data right now:

A. Today's date = _____

B. The date you opened your Etsy shop for business = _____

C. The number of feedbacks you have received = _____ (the count, not the percent)

D. The percentage of your feedback that is positive = _____

E. The number of items you have for sale in your shop = _____

F. The number of items you have sold in your shop = _____

G. The number of shop hearts you have received = _____ (not your item hearts, only the hearts for your shop)

H. The number of views for all the items for sale in your shop (add them all up or make an estimate) = _____

Seven Etsy Shop Ratios (Stories)

Following are seven stories you can find in your Etsy shop that reveal something unique about your business. If your shop has just recently opened, you should wait at least three months before performing these calculations. It is also helpful to look at these ratios once or twice every year and compare them to see whether the trends are moving up or down or staying consistent. You can also set goals for these ratios and see whether certain behaviors improve them. The longer your shop has been in business, the more precise and accurate these ratios become. Ratios are not magic and might not always tell the full story. These ratios provide the best analysis when you ask these questions: Why did this happen? What caused this to be so high (or low)? What can I do to improve this story? There is no right or wrong ratio. Every Etsy seller has different ratios for different reasons. Knowing your business gives you the best ability to manage your business toward success. Remember, you can also calculate these ratios for your competitors or Etsy shops you admire and learn from them, too. Don't obsess about following your ratios; they are only one of many tools for evaluating your business.

Inventory Cycles (I)

This ratio tells you how many times (on average) you have sold all the items in your shop. It is found by taking the number of items you have sold in your shop (F) and dividing it by the number of items you have for sale in your shop (E). For example, you have made 1,000 sales and currently have 20 items for sale in your shop—1,000 sales divided by 20 items equals 50. This Etsy shop has sold all the items listed in its shop 50 times. If all of these were unique items, this Etsy shop's customers would have seen the inventory cycle 50 times. A *cycle* is when all the items listed in a shop are eventually sold. This does not mean that all 20 items were listed and then sold until there were 0 items listed, because new items are typically being added when old items are being sold. This ratio can be skewed if you have an atypically large or small number of items for sale in your shop. Calculate your ratio and put your number in the blanks: My inventory has sold, on average, ____ times. I've sold everything in my shop ____ times. If I sell one-of-a-kind (OOAK) originals, my customers have seen completely new inventory in my shop ____ times. Generally, the more times you sell your entire inventory, the better, but if you have a really high number, you might want to consider listing more items in your shop, so you are not constantly having to show a new batch of inventory.

Days to Cycle Inventory

This ratio tells you how long it typically takes for your inventory to complete a cycle, or sell everything you have listed. It is found by taking the number of days your shop has been open and dividing that by the answer you just calculated in the preceding inventory cycles (I). The number of days your shop has been open can be found by taking today's date (A) and subtracting the date you opened your shop for business (B). The number of days your shop has been open does not have to be exact if that is too much counting for you—an estimate will do just fine to get the general story. For example, your Etsy shop has been open for about four years, or 1,460 days (365 times 4), and your inventory has cycled 50 times. The average number of days it takes to cycle the inventory is 29.2 days (1,460 days divided by 50 inventory cycles). This means that, on average, all inventory is listed and then sold in about a month. Calculate your ratio and put your numbers in the blanks: On average, my Etsy shop takes ____ days to sell my entire inventory. If I don't create and list any new products, my listed inventory will be depleted in ____ days. Customers will have to wait ____ days to see a brand-new batch of inventory listed. Generally, the lower this ratio the better, but if you are selling out of your inventory too fast, it might be a sign that you cannot keep up with the demand for your inventory and need to hire help or look for efficiencies in the production of new inventory.

Heart to Sales Ratio (J)

The heart to sales ratio is one of my favorite Etsy ratios. The heart to sales ratio tells you how many hearts your shop typically receives before you make a sale. This ratio is found by taking how many hearts your shop has received (G) divided by the number of sales you have made in your shop (F). For example, you have 2,000 shop hearts and you have made 500 sales. The heart to sales ratio is 4.0 (2,000 hearts divided by 500 sales). This means that, on average, it takes four Etsy customers to heart your shop before one of them (or another customer) makes a purchase from the shop. The heart to sales ratio is not a magic guarantee to make more sales. Instead, it shows a relationship between one action (having a popular Etsy shop that receives a heart, or favorite) and your Etsy shop making a sale. Some Etsy sellers think this ratio is nonsense, while others see it as a good predictor of future sales. I believe that this ratio is consistent for most Etsy sellers when looking at trends over a longer period of time. This ratio tends to stay constant and within a specific range for each Etsy seller, although I believe each shop will have a different range for this ratio number. Shops that are admired by many and have more highly priced products might need 20 hearts to eventually see a sale, and shops that sell something that is popular with a low price might need only three hearts to receive a sale. Hearts do not directly cause sales, but there is a relationship worth recognizing. Hearts show the popularity of a product and shop, and more popular products and shops typically see more sales. Calculate your ratio and put your number in the blanks: My shop typically receives ____ hearts before making a sale. I should roughly make my next sale when ____ more customers heart my shop. I need ____ more customers to find my shop before someone will make a purchase from my shop. Generally, the lower this ratio the better, because it takes fewer new customers to find your shop and to eventually make a purchase. However, realize that *sales* are the ultimate goals, not artificial hearts.

Feedback Response Ratio

The feedback response ratio shows you how many of your customers who make purchases come back to your shop and provide you with positive feedback. It is found by taking the number of feedback responses you have received (C) divided by the total number of sales your shop has made (F). For example, an Etsy shop has received 1,000 positive feedbacks and has made 1,500 sales. The feedback response ratio is 66.67 percent (1,000 feedbacks divided by 1,500 sales). This means that 66.67 percent of all your customers typically come back to your shop and provide you feedback. If you purchase a lot of items on Etsy, this ratio can be influenced by all the feedbacks your shop receives from making those purchases. This could even artificially put this ratio over 100 percent. If you want to eliminate this bias in the ratio, you can subtract the number of feedbacks you have received as a buyer from the number of feedbacks received. Calculate your ratio and put your number in the blanks: After customers purchase an item, there is a ____ percent chance that they will come back and leave positive feedback for my shop. ____ percent of my customers leave me feedback. Generally, the higher this ratio the better, because it is proof that your customers are satisfied and also that positive feedback encourages future customers to make purchases from your shop. I believe that the more engaged and familiar customers are with Etsy, the greater the chance that they will provide feedback. Some customers (especially first-time Etsy buyers) might not even realize they have the opportunity to provide feedback.

Sales per Day Ratio (K)

The sales per day ratio tells you how many sales your shop makes on a typical day. It is found by taking the number of sales your shop has received (F) divided by the number of days your shop has been open (the number of days between when you opened your shop for business and today's date). For example, an Etsy shop has 1,000 sales and has been open for 200 days. The number of sales per day, on average, is five (1,000 sales divided by 200 days). This means that on a typical day, this Etsy shop makes five sales. This ratio can also be a decimal number. For example, an Etsy shop has 100 sales and has been open 300 days. The number of sales per day, on average, is 0.33 (100 sales divided by 300 days). In this case, on a typical day, this Etsy shop makes one-third of a sale every day (or the equivalent of a sale every three days). To find the number of days it takes to make a sale, divide 1 by the decimal (1 divided by 0.33 equals 3 days). This ratio is an average, but it gives you a good idea of whether your Etsy shop is performing above or below average in numbers of sales you are making. If you typically make one sale per day, but have a day in which you sell five items, you know your shop is performing five times better than average. The opposite is also true: If you typically sell one item per day and don't make any sales for seven days, you know you are in a slight sales slump and might need to take action via promotions to jump-start activity. Calculate your ratio and put your number in the blanks: My shop typically makes ____ sales in one day. Today, if my shop performs as it has historically, I should make ____ sales. Generally, the higher this ratio the better, because you are making more sales. If your number is a decimal, aim for making one sale per day as a goal. This ratio will always be historical for the entire life of your shop. This means that if your shop has been open for two years and has received very little business during those two years, but you are now operating your shop with renewed vigor (making more frequent sales), this ratio will be understated.

Average Product Views

This ratio shows how many views your average product listing has received. It is found by taking the total number of views of all the items listed in your shop (H) divided by the number of items for sale in your shop (E). For example, an Etsy shop has 10,000 views of all its products and has 50 items listed for sale. The average number of product views is 200 (10,000 views divided by 50 products). This means that when a specific individual product listing has 200 views, it is at the shop average for number of views. If a product has 600 views, you know it is attracting a lot more attention (600 divided by 200 equals 3 times more attention) than the average product. This ratio is influenced by items in your shop that have been listed for years (and thus have acquired a lot more views through that time period) in conjunction with newly listed items that have acquired very few views. This is why this ratio is an average and a guideline. It is useful to look at which products get the most views compared to others and to try to figure out why they are getting more traffic (keywords, picture quality, price, color, etc.), then to apply these similar characteristics to other products. Calculate your ratio and put your number in the blanks: Each item in my Etsy shop typically receives ____ views. Each one of my products has been seen ____ times by customers. Not all views are created equal, and I would desire a high-quality view to a one-second glance any day of the week. Generally, the more views, the better the chance an item will sell and the more exposure your shop is receiving. The more exposure for your product, the better the chance it will eventually sell. Views are not sales, but you need views to sell an item.

Average Shop Hearts (L)

This ratio shows you how many shop hearts your Etsy shop receives on the typical day. It is found by taking the number of shop hearts your Etsy business has received (G) divided by the number of days your shop has been open (number of days between the opening date of your shop and today's date). For example, you have 2,000 shop hearts and have had your business open for 500 days. The average shop hearts is 4.0 (2,000 hearts divided by 500 days). This means that, on the average day, four Etsy shoppers will favorite (or heart) your shop. The higher this number is, the more popular your shop is with customers. Calculate your ratio and put your number in the blanks: On a typical day, ____ Etsy shoppers heart my shop. Today, I will receive approximately ____ shop hearts. Generally, the higher this number the better, because it shows that your shop is seeing many new shoppers and that they are telling you they like your products and business. This number is not your bottom-line goal of sales. Realize that many Etsy sellers will heart a shop for various reasons, not all of which mean they will come back to your shop and eventually make a purchase.

Three Etsy Shop Forecasts (Predictions)

Following are three ratios that attempt to forecast or predict future activities for your business. The one certain thing is that forecasts will be wrong (just ask a weather forecaster, economist, or financial planner), but knowing the forecast is typically better than knowing nothing at all! These forecasts are mathematically valid on which to base your expectations, but the actual results will usually be better or worse than expected.

Hearts to Cycle Inventory Predictor

This predicting ratio forecasts how many hearts you need to cycle, or sell, the entire inventory you currently have listed. It is found by taking the preceding heart to sales ratio (J) and multiplying that number by how many items you currently have listed in your shop (E). For example, your heart to sales ratio is 4.0, and you have 30 items listed in your shop. It is forecast that when your shop receives 120 more shop hearts (4.0 heart to sales ratio times 30 items), most of the products listed in your shop currently will be sold. This number can give you a target or goal to watch in shop hearts that are being received by your business. Calculate your ratio and put your number in the blanks: It is forecast that when my shop receives _____ more shop hearts, I will have sold all items in my shop. In order to cycle or sell all of my existing inventory (and history is a good predictor of the future), I need _____ Etsy shoppers to heart my shop, which will hopefully lead directly to sales, if the heart to sales ratio maintains a consistent relationship. Generally, you want this number to be lower, but realize it is just an estimated guess at predicting future outcomes of your business.

Next Sale Predictor

This predicting ratio estimates the number of days until your next sale. It is found by taking the number 1 and dividing it by the preceding average sales per day ratio (K). For example, the average sales per day ratio is 5 (1 divided by 5 sales per day ratio equals 0.20). This means that it forecast to take one-fifth of a day (20 percent of a 24-hour day), or 4.8 hours (0.20 times 24 hours), until you make your next sale. Let's look at another example, where the average sales per day ratio is a decimal (0.33)—1 divided by 0.33 sales per day ratio equals 3. This means that it is forecast to take three days to make the next sale. Don't count on this forecast being accurate, but it can give you a benchmark to which to compare your actual performance. If this ratio forecasts that your next sale will come in one day, but you have not received a sale in 10 days, something is wrong, and your shop is experiencing a slowdown. Calculate your ratio and put your number in the blank: It is forecast that I will make my next sale in ____days (hours) if historical conditions continue. Generally, you should want your next sale to be sooner rather than later!

Next Shop Heart Predictor

This predicting ratio estimates how many hours it takes for you to receive your next shop heart. It is found by taking the number 24 (hours) and dividing it by the previously calculated average shop heart ratio (L). For example, an Etsy shop has an average shop heart ratio of 4.0, and 24 divided by 4 is 6. In this case, it should be expected that in six hours, another Etsy seller will heart, or favorite, your shop. Calculate your ratio and put your number in the blanks: I should expect my next shop heart in ____ hours. On average, every ____ hours, a new Etsy shopper will not only find my shop, but provide feedback to me that he or she likes my shop. Generally, the sooner someone is forecast to heart your shop, the better.

Download: Etsy Shop Ratio Calculator

Use this tool to enter your eight pieces of data and calculate your ratios. You can also track these ratios through time to see whether your ratios are trending favorably or unfavorably.

Note: To download this document, please go to www.etsy-preneurship.com/downloads.

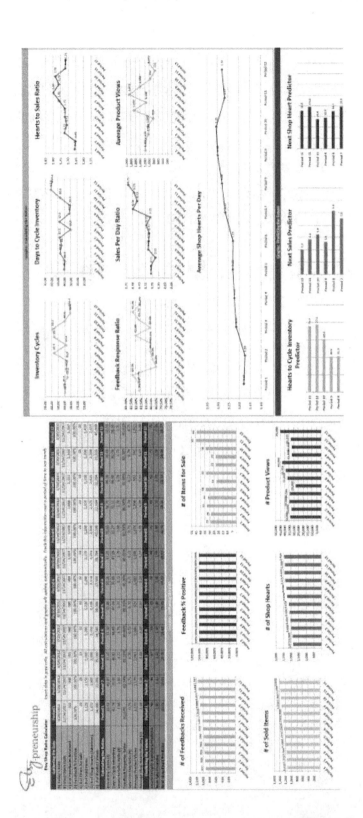

Advanced Application External Study

Etsy Marketplace Trends That Impact Your Business

Your Etsy business is part of the greater Etsy marketplace. By knowing your marketplace inside and out, you can gain some key advantages to helping your Etsy shop thrive! First, having a good feel for where your business stands in the greater Etsy community gives you a broader perspective. When handmade artists sell at a craft show, they typically walk around getting a good feel for the craft show (the quality of products, the people there, the selling prices, the types of discounts being offered, and what type of goods are being sold). This survey helps you realize your unique place in the "Etsy craft show." In the same way, looking at trends in the general Etsy marketplace allows you to see how your business fits in the bigger picture. Second, knowing the general trends in the Etsy marketplace allows you to have a competitive advantage over other sellers. If you spot a significant new trend in the Etsy marketplace, it allows you to act before other sellers do. Being a first responder gives you a competitive advantage and a head start to make changes in your Etsy shop that will help you ride the wave of change that is sweeping through the marketplace. Third, knowing key trends helps you be an informed business owner and make better decisions for your business. There can be a general trend happening on Etsy that you, as one seller on Etsy, can choose to join or ignore. In the financial markets, people sometimes say, "Buy this stock— it is so valuable and will really make lots of money for you," while a few others are quietly selling all they own of that stock because they think the tide is about to change. Knowledge is power when it comes to making decisions and running your business.

Etsy Weather Reports

Every month, Etsy is kind enough to provide an article on its blog that gives Etsy sellers insight into the greater Etsy marketplace. Etsy calls these the "Weather Reports." The first Weather Report was published in September of 2007 and has been consistently posted since then. In these weather reports, only five data points are tracked, but these five data points reveal a lot about the state of the

Etsy marketplace and significant trends that are occurring. These reports are popular with Etsy sellers and always generate some discussion every month when they are released. I always enjoy looking at these reports and have been tracking them for years in a spreadsheet I built to analyze the trends. Now I get to share my analytical findings with you.

The Weather Report Study

In order to trust the interpretation of the data, you need to trust the study. In this study, I gathered all five data points (goods sold in dollars, the number of items sold, the number of new items listed, the number of new members joined, and the number of total page views on Etsy) from each month's Weather Report and put them in a spreadsheet for a period of 60 months, or five years (February 2007 through February 2012). Data was not present for eight of these months, and I interpolated the data as a best estimate for consistent analysis. I then studied the relationship between these five variables by looking at the 10 ratios from which it is possible to find stories and trends hidden in the data. Next, I explored to see whether there were any monthly and annual growth rate stories and seasonality trends. From there, I explored some very rough estimates at revenue levels, marketplace wages and efficiency, and daily and by-the-minute statistics. Now I can provide my opinions about what I see in Etsy's future. The spreadsheet I used for this analysis, which is available for download on Etsy-preneurship.com, allows you to see how every number was calculated and helps you gain trust in the analysis and interpretation of the data. Having access to this data also allows you to perform your own analysis and interpretation on the Etsy marketplace. I suggest you have the data and graphs at your fingertips while you go through this part of the book. The graphics will help you in your understanding of the Etsy marketplace.

Weather Report Trends

These five categories are the data points revealed directly in the Weather Reports and show the amazing growth Etsy has encountered during the past five years. Let's explore each of these in depth to learn more about the Etsy marketplace.

Goods Sold

The dollar value of goods sold by Etsy sellers is made up from the revenue of thousands of Etsy sellers each month. Growth for the value in dollars of goods sold appears to be growing exponentially. Exponential growth is not typically sustainable, yet it shows the meteoric rise in Etsy popularity during the past five years. In February of 2007, about $1 million in total goods was sold on Etsy; five years later, a whopping $58.3 million was sold. Each month, the value of goods sold has increased on average by $955,000. This is a promising trend if you sell on Etsy, because each month, there is more revenue to capture. Today, Etsy sellers bring home $58.3 million in revenue every month. During the typical month, this number grows by 7.6 percent from the previous month, so this could be a target for your Etsy shop if you desire to keep up with Etsy's growth. I believe that a good part of this growth comes from shops that are growing their monthly revenue, but also realize that this number is influenced by the sheer number of new sellers joining Etsy each month. The average annual growth is 127.6 percent. Etsy enables a lot of Etsy sellers to bring home solid revenue numbers.

Items Sold

This data point tracks how many items are sold on Etsy each month by count. Growth in this category is also very strong. In February of 2007, there were

273,043 sales transactions. This jumped to 2,869,606 transactions by February 2012. Each month, an additional 43,276 additional items are sold on Etsy, on average. The growth rate for the typical month is 4.5 percent, and average annual growth in items sold is 80.3 percent. The number of items sold is increasing at a slightly slower pace than the value of the goods sold. Each November and December, a peak in items sold occurs due to the typical retail seasonality around Christmastime. Etsy sellers call this time of year the "holiday rush," and preparations begin many months earlier. November and December sales can push an Etsy shop into having a fantastic year.

New Items Listed

This data point tracks how many new items Etsy sellers are listing for sale in all of the Etsy shops. This number shows how full or empty the shelves are in the Etsy marketplace. In February of 2007, there were 148,422 new items listed for sale on Etsy. Five years later, this number grew to more than 2,240,945 new items listed. During this five-year period, in a typical month, there were 34,875 new creations made and listed by Etsy sellers— that is a lot of creativity! The average monthly growth rate is 5.3 percent, and the annual growth rate comes in at 78.9 percent. For some reason, you can see that after November 2010, the number of new items listed each month dropped significantly, but it has been rising steadily since then, and the general trend has been a steady rise.

New Members Joined

Each month, thousands of new customers and sellers join the Etsy community to become part of the handmade, vintage, and supply movement that is Etsy. In February 2007, there were 22,392 new members, and in February 2012, there were 654,501 new members who joined Etsy! This is a lot of new potential customers and is one of the most exciting trends for an Etsy seller to see happening. Every time a new person joins Etsy, he or she has made the leap from not knowing about Etsy to knowing about Etsy—and most likely purchasing something new on Etsy. While customers are customers for your shop, they are also general customers of Etsy. Getting new customers to recognize and trust your business is a difficult first step to cross, and once people make their first purchase on Etsy, they are likely to come back for more in the future. Many of these new members are experiencing handmade, vintage, and supplies for the first time. During this five-year period, on a typical month, 10,535 new members joined per month. This is a 6.5 percent average monthly growth rate and a 94.8 percent average annual growth rate. The number of new members joining has recently encountered a significant spike. Growth in new members is encouraging.

Page Views

Every page that someone looks at on Etsy is tracked and counted, and this data point shows how much shopping and browsing occurs on Etsy each month. In 2007, there were about 163 million page views a month, and this has jumped to a staggering 1.3 billion page views per month. Traffic has increased by 4.3 percent, on average, each month, and annual growth is around 60.4 percent. This is the lowest growth rate among all five Weather Report data points, but it also appears to have the fewest peaks and valleys (i.e., the most consistency in growth). During the past five years, this steady driver has seen an average monthly increase of almost 19 million page views.

Weather Report Ratios

Most of the Etsy sellers who are consistent readers of the monthly Weather Reports will be able to tell you that the general trends of the preceding five data points (goods sold, items sold, new items listed, new members joined, and page views) are all going up almost all the time, but the following stories are not as well known. These stories are revealed by looking at the relationship between these five numbers. Some are more revealing and useful than others, but all tell us more of the story line of the Etsy marketplace. Each of these ratios is simply taking one of the data points and dividing it by the other data points. Let's explore these 10 stories to learn new things about the Etsy marketplace.

Good Sold per Items Sold

This very telling story shows that Etsy customers are buying increasingly higher-priced items on Etsy. The average price of an item sold in 2007 was $9.45 and has risen to $19.68 in 2011. The average purchase has grown more than twice as large over the past five years! If all other things were held constant, this price would generally increase at the pace of inflation, but it has grown much faster. This means that Etsy sellers and customers are making and buying higher-priced items. With this information, you can compare how your prices for your products compare to the average of $19.68. Are your prices well above or well below that figure? If you are far away from this average, how will this influence your marketing?

Goods Sold per New Items Listed

This story adds light to the increasing average selling price of an item. During 2011, the average selling price of a new item listed was higher than the average selling price of an item sold. Etsy sellers appear to be more comfortable listing higher-priced items, or they are listing fewer products and selling more higher-priced items. Prices of new listings will eventually influence the average price of a product sold.

Goods Sold per New Members Joined

Over the past five years, the following positive trend has held true: The more members who join, the more they and all customers purchase. Not all of these sales increases are from the new members, but over the five-year period, the relationship exists that if a new person joins Etsy, Etsy will experience an average increase in total sales of $82.45. The more new members, the better Etsy and Etsy sellers typically perform.

Goods Sold per Page Views

Everyone knows that page views are valuable. Etsy sellers want more views of their products, because it increases the chance that the item will eventually find the right customers and sell. This ratio assigns a value to the typical page view. Over the five-year period, page views are becoming more valuable (from around $0.01 per page view in 2007 to $0.04 in 2011). Perform this experiment: Take the number of page views your Etsy shop receives in a month, multiply it by $0.04, and compare that amount to how much revenue you received. For example, your Etsy shop had 4,000 page views during one month and had total revenue of $1,000; multiply 4,000 page views times $0.04 and you get $160, or the estimated average revenue per page view. This $160 compared to the actual $1,000 in revenue is much lower. This means this Etsy shop's revenue per page view was 6.25 times higher than the Etsy average ($1,000 divided by $160). Does your Etsy shop consistently underperform or outperform the average? Is your Etsy shop's revenue per page view consistent? If it is, you can back into the calculation to find out how many page views your Etsy shop needs to meet a certain revenue target. Page views are consistently more valuable in the month of December, if you want to target your promotions to drive traffic to your Etsy shop.

Items Sold per New Items Listed

This ratio, which hovers around the number 1, tells the story of whether all new items listed will eventually sell. When the ratio is below 1.0, more items are being listed on Etsy than are selling each month (i.e., Etsy inventory levels are getting larger). When the ratio is above 1.0, more items are being sold than new items are being listed (i.e., Etsy inventory levels are getting smaller). The recent trend is that more items have been selling than new items are being listed—a great opportunity for Etsy sellers to create more products and place them in the marketplace. I believe this ratio will move back and forth over periods of years. The current trend (above 1.0) is a result of the new listings growing so quickly (below 1.0) for numerous years. Through time, this ratio should trend toward 1.0 as new listings eventually sell. When the ratio is below 1.0, realize that the competition for sales of new items is more intense.

Items Sold per New Members Joined

This relationship has been fairly steady over the past five years. Typically, the Etsy marketplace can expect about five items to sell for every new member who joins. This does not mean that every new member will purchase five items, but that the relationship is steady. If new members join at a faster pace than the number of items sold increases, this ratio will eventually drop, as it did in late 2011. Again, new members are a key driver in the Etsy marketplace's performance.

Items Sold per Page Views

This ratio answers the question, "How many page views, on average, does it take to sell a product?" In 2007, it took around 744 page views to sell an average item. In 2011, it took only around 494 page views to sell an item. Of course, not all page views on Etsy consist of people looking at products. Page views can also consist of people viewing forums, blogs, homepages, and profiles. Really, the average item sells in less than 494 views, but you can use this as a point of comparison. If you have an item that has received more than 494 views and not yet sold, you know this item is taking more views than the Etsy average to sell, and you can act accordingly to try and help the item sell.

New Items Listed per New Members Joined

For every new member who joins Etsy, there are a select number of items for this customer to shop for. This ratio tells us how many new items are available for each new member to view. From 2007 to 2010, this ratio was very consistent, hovering around eight new items listed per new member, but has dropped to around four new items listed per new member starting in 2011. This means that the more new inventory you list on Etsy, the less competition there will be than previously, which spells opportunity for Etsy sellers.

Page Views per New Items Listed

This ratio tells a similar story as the preceding ratio (new items listed per new member joined). New inventory that is listed now is easier to find than it was previously, meaning that the chance of any random page view being of your newly listed item is greater. This ratio used to hover around 400 page views per new items listed, but has jumped to 600 page views per new item listed—a better chance that you newly listed inventory will be viewed.

Page Views per New Members Joined

This ratio has been getting consistently lower over the five-year period, telling us that new members are not typically looking at as many pages as they used to. This might also reveal that new members are more quickly finding what they want to buy and not having to view as many pages before making their purchase. This is very likely, because Etsy has consistently been working on improving the search capabilities (it has recently moved to a relevancy-based search instead of its historical recency-based search).

Etsy Seasonality

Just as there are four seasons in a year, the Etsy marketplace has its ups and downs throughout the year. Some months are slower than others, but overall, Etsy always has lots of activity. Over the past five years, 36.3 percent of a year's goods sold in dollars come in the last three months of the year (October, November, and December). This is the typical retail rush period and Etsy experiences it, too. Seasonality is unique for the Etsy marketplace, because almost every month experiences positive growth. Most Etsy sellers should experience a jump in sales during the last three months of the year, but these growth opportunities do not happen without work. Do not assume that the holiday rush will benefit your business if you don't put yourself out there with specific marketing campaigns, advertising opportunities, and promotions.

Revenue Estimates

Etsy sellers make revenue, Etsy makes revenue, and PayPal makes revenue, and I am happy for everyone to have high revenues! All three groups need each other to benefit, and when an Etsy seller wins, so does Etsy. When Etsy wins, Etsy sellers eventually win, too. These are estimates of revenues generated by Etsy, PayPal, and all Etsy sellers. The one thing I can tell you about these estimates is that they are not accurate—they are only estimates with many assumptions—but they still can tell us some interesting things about the Etsy marketplace.

The Weather Reports tell us how many dollars of goods are sold each month as well as how many new items are listed. The following two data points give us a starting point to look at the revenues that Etsy and PayPal could receive from these activities relating to Etsy transactions.

- *Etsy revenue estimate for February 2012.* Some of Etsy's revenue comes from listing fees ($0.20 per listing) and a sales percentage fee (3.5 percent of a sold item's value). In February 2012, Etsy stated that there were 2,240,945 new items listed. If each of these new items listed generated $0.20 in listing fees, then $448,189 of revenue was generated for Etsy (2,240,945 new items times $0.20). Also, $58.3 million in goods were sold in February, earning an estimated $2,040,500 in revenue for Etsy ($58.3 million in sales times 3.5 percent). This gives us an estimated $2,488,689 in revenue for Etsy in February. This does not account for fees that were never paid by Etsy sellers. Etsy has never clearly stated its definition of "new item listed." This number might or might not include renewals of products. In addition, Etsy has not disclosed all of its revenue streams. This merely helps you see that

Etsy had revenues of roughly $2,488,689 in February. When you compare this $2.5 million in revenue to the $58.3 million in revenue generated for Etsy sellers, Etsy sellers are the big winners!

- *PayPal revenue estimates for February 2012 (Etsy-related).* If you assume all transactions that take place on Etsy use PayPal (which they do not), we can estimate how much revenue PayPal generates from Etsy transactions during a month. If you assume PayPal charges $0.30 per transaction plus a 2.9 percent sales fee, it is estimated that PayPal generated $2,551,581.80 in revenue in February ($58.3 million sales times 2.9 percent plus 2,869,606 transactions times $.030). One interesting thing to notice is that Etsy's estimated revenue and PayPal's estimated revenue from these Etsy transactions are almost equal. PayPal and Etsy might benefit equally from the success of Etsy sellers. Etsy has now made "Direct Checkout" available to Etsy sellers, giving sellers the ability to accept credit card payments through Etsy that will be paid out into Etsy seller's bank account. This will eventually drive some of PayPal's profits to Etsy.

Etsy Wages and Efficiency

If you take the preceding revenue estimates for February 2012 and divide those by 29 days and then 24 hours in a day, you can estimate how much revenue is generated per hour. Etsy made an estimated $3,575.70 per hour during February. All Etsy sellers brought home $83,764.37 per hour! This $83,764.37 is shared among thousands of Etsy sellers, but the amount is quite large! Individual Etsy sellers brought in about 23.4 times more revenue per hour than Etsy as a whole ($83,764.37 divided by $3,575.70). This multiple of 23.4 shows how efficient Etsy is at helping Etsy sellers achieve success. Back in 2007, this ratio was around 16.0. This means that Etsy is becoming more efficient at helping Etsy sellers achieve their goals of running small businesses. Let's hope this trend continues.

Day-by-Day Statistics

Here are some simple statistics to help you get a better idea of what Etsy looks like on a typical day in February 2012 compared to one in February 2007.

- $2,010,345 in goods sold per day in February 2012 compared to only $35,714 in February 2007
- 98,952 items sold in 2012 compared to only 9,752 in 2007
- 77,274 new items listed in 2012 compared to 5,301 in 2007
- 22,569 new members on a typical day in 2012 compared to 800 in 2007
- 44,827,586 page views in 2012 compared to 5,818,121 in 2007

Today is a good day to be an Etsy seller!

In an "Etsy" Minute

Here are some simple statistics to help you get a better idea of what one minute of activity looks like on Etsy in February 2012 compared to one in February 2007.

- In one minute in February 2012, $1,396 worth of goods was sold. In February 2007, only $25.00 worth of goods was sold.

- In February 2012, 69 items were sold. In February 2007, only seven items were sold.
- In the same time period in 2012, 54 new items were listed. In 2007, only four items were listed.
- In February 2012, almost 16 new members per minute joined Etsy. In February 2007, not quite one new member per minute joined.
- In one minute in February 2012, 31,130 Etsy pages were viewed. In February 2007, only 4,040 pages were viewed.

The Future of Etsy?

I've been watching the Etsy marketplace for many years, as both a seller and a customer. I've tracked Weather Report trends, read the blogs, and talked with thousands of Etsy sellers and customers. I've talked about Etsy with people who are familiar with the site and those who have never heard of it. Etsy has been a significant part of my life, and here is my opinion about where Etsy is headed in the future:

- Handmade has not caught on like it could in the larger economy. Growth opportunities abound. Customers will continue purchasing more everyday items and gifts on Etsy.

- Etsy makes entrepreneurship more easily attainable for the average person than ever before. Growth opportunities abound. More individuals will open new businesses on Etsy, and more existing Etsy sellers will continue to open additional Etsy shops.
- Etsy will continue to grow globally, expanding into more countries and deepening its presence in these countries.
- Etsy has by no means reached its peak in the "cool and practical" category. Many years ago, people did not have smartphones, but now many people have them because they are both cool and practical. As a marketplace, Etsy not only includes a cool factor but also serves many practical needs.
- Many people I talk to still have not heard about Etsy, but when they learn about it, most of them like it. Market growth opportunities are still large.

- Etsy is not a company to stand still. Change will happen. Some of it will be good and some bad. Etsy sellers hope the change is positive. I believe Etsy will begin marketing itself as more of a resource to the entrepreneurs it serves.
- Etsy might or might not go public at some point (i.e., choose to be listed on the stock market). Right now, I think Etsy is holding off because it likes where it stands and can call all its own shots without having to worry about shareholders. I also think Etsy does not have enough revenue, diversified revenue streams, and profits to seriously entertain the thought right now. The more Etsy grows, the greater the chance of its going public. Going public is not a business's main goal or purpose.
- In May 2012, Etsy became a Certified B Corporation™ (a rigorously certified corporation), which sets high standards regarding employees, the community, and environmental interests. Etsy has used this certification to better define itself. Profit is, of course, one motive for

Etsy's actions, but other motives are driving its actions as well. I believe this is good for Etsy sellers, because it is not about taking every penny of profit available from the sellers, but also about making sure sellers are able to make more sales.

- In May 2012, Etsy had an additional funding of $40 million from its investors. With this round of funding, the market current appears to be valuing the worth of Etsy at approximately $600 to $700 million. This funding should continue to provide opportunities for growth.
- Etsy sellers sometimes grumble and complain, but generally an Etsy seller's happiness with Etsy is in direct correlation to the profits he or she receives. Most Etsy sellers will continue to be happy as long as they are profitable.

I wish Etsy and Etsy sellers both the best! Etsy serves a great need, and I look forward to a future that appears to be full of opportunity.

Download: Etsy Weather Reports Analysis

For your review, the download includes every data point and calculation that was used in this chapter's analysis. Please use this raw data as an opportunity to create your own interpretation of the trends. Any time data is shared in a graph, there can be various interpretations. I hope I have helped you see Etsy in a way that you never have seen Etsy before!

Note: To download this document, please go to www.etsy-preneurship.com/downloads.

Download Details and Closing Thoughts

The downloadable tools for each chapter can be accessed two ways:

1. Etsy-preneurship.com—Each chapter of the book has a corresponding web page with additional commentary, videos, and a link to access the downloads.

2. www.etsy-preneurship.com/downloads—All downloads are also available on this page.

When prompted, enter the password: Etsyshopthrive (no spaces, capitalized E).

For download system compatibility, please see Chapter 1's Instructions for Etsy-preneurship.com and Accessing Digital Downloads.

If you have enjoyed this book, I want to hear from you. If you have follow-up questions, I want to hear from you. If you have a success story, I want to hear from you. Do you get it? I want to hear from you! Here are the easiest ways for us to stay in touch:

- Visit Etsy-preneurship.com and take in all the additional chapters' contents and make sure to sign up for the e-mail list so we can stay connected.

- Visit my two Etsy shops, JJMFinance and Epreneurship. I've put together a special package of all the Etsy business resources that I have created for Etsy sellers through the years specifically for Etsy-preneurship readers.
- Follow, like, and connect with me on social media (Facebook, Twitter, Pinterest, and others).
- Tell other Etsy sellers about this book. Through the years, I have relied on Etsy sellers' word of mouth recommendations to spread my knowledge, services, and tools. Spread the word in your Etsy teams, suggest my book in the Etsy forums, blog about your experience with this book, write a good review on sites where books are sold, and share about it on social media. This book is for the Etsy community and I need your help to make it a success. I have put my all into this book and I appreciate your grassroots effort to spread the word.
- Find out how you can get a one-on-one personal business consultation with me or have me speak at your

handmade/small business engagement on the "Contact" section of <u>Etsy-preneurship.com</u>.

- Go and practice Etsy-preneurship! Each of us helps make Etsy a better marketplace and reshapes the global economy.

CPSIA information can be obtained
at www.ICGtesting.com
Printed in the USA
BVHW082243070621
608941BV00002B/421